The Idiom
of Contemporary Thought

The Idiom of Contemporary Thought

A Reinterpretation
of some of the Problems
to which it gives rise

by

CRAWFORD KNOX

GREENWOOD PRESS, PUBLISHERS
WESTPORT, CONNECTICUT

The Library of Congress has catalogued this publication as follows:

Library of Congress Cataloging in Publication Data

Knox, Crawford.
    The idiom of contemporary thought, a reinterpretation of some of the problems to which it gives rise.

    Reprint of the 1956 ed. published by Chapman & Hall, London.
        Bibliography: p.
        1. Philosophy. I. Title.
    B1646.K745313 1973   190   72-11479
    ISBN 0-8371-6672-1

TO MY WIFE

Originally published in 1956
by Chapman & Hall, London

Reprinted with the permission
of Chapman & Hall Ltd.

First Greenwood Reprinting 1973

Library of Congress Catalogue Card Number 72-11479

ISBN 0-8371-6672-1

Printed in the United States of America

PREFACE

THIS book draws evidence from many fields of know-ledge and experience, in none of which am I a specialist: indeed no one could be a specialist in them all. Yet each of them is relevant to what I have to say, and so I have had recourse to works by authorities who have seen their subjects in a wide perspective and have expressed their findings in a form intelligible to a layman. I hope that I have selected reasonably from such books as were available and that I have not so distorted what they say that my main contentions will be prejudiced.

The general thesis, however (as distinct from the subjects from which I draw my evidence), derives from no such authorities. I have read a substantial number of works by contemporary philosophers, but what I have learned from them, with several important exceptions, has helped me to clarify my thoughts and understand the problems whose answers I was seeking, rather than to forward my argument as such. Nor does it benefit as much as it might from the classical philosophers.

I am acutely aware that a more complete understanding of what they said would have helped me to take further some of the problems considered in these essays, for these have been of perennial interest to mankind. Even for the purposes of exposition, the well-placed analogy with Kant or with Spinoza might often have illuminated what I wished to say. That such comparisons might profitably be drawn will be readily apparent to any philosopher who may read the book. Indeed, I was deeply encouraged to realize, when most of my own ideas had already been formulated, just how close many of them were to those of Spinoza, notwithstanding his utterly different approach.

Yet for two reasons I have hesitated to make such comparisons in these essays. The first reason is that, although I hope the book will prove to be of interest to philosophers, I have striven so to clarify my thought and language that it will be intelligible to laymen. For them such comparisons would not be very helpful and might even impede the argument.

My second reason is that I feel my knowledge to be insufficient to enable me safely to draw such analogies. This is particularly true with Spinoza, for his system is so closely argued and interdependent one part with another, that it is necessary to understand it as a whole, together with its seventeenth century background. I find the same difficulty, though perhaps to a somewhat lesser extent, with all the other great philosophers.

The thesis I have to propound I have set out, as clearly and briefly as I could, in the form of two essays. These will, I hope, be suggestive of new lines of thought. Perhaps, if opportunity offers in the little spare time that is left to a Civil Servant, it may be possible elsewhere for me to explore more fully the implications of their theme.

I would like to express my appreciation to those of my friends who read the book at the various stages in its development and endured discussion of the problems which it raised. I would also like to thank Professor Dingle, Professor Leon, and Professor H. D. Lewis for reading parts of the manuscript in its early stages. I owe a particular debt to Professor H. H. Price, who helped me greatly to remove some flaws from the argument and to improve its presentation. And I have especial reason to be grateful to my wife, whose help and encouragement have been unfailing,

C. K.

Shalford, Surrey.
  January 1956.

'They reason excellently in the idiom of their beliefs, but they cannot reason outside, or against, their beliefs because they have no other idiom in which to express their thoughts.'

Witchcraft, Oracles and Magic among the Azande, by E. E. Evans-Pritchard.

We shall not cease from exploration
And the end of all our exploring
Will be to arrive where we started
And know the place for the first time.

Little Gidding, by T. S. Eliot.

CONTENTS

Part I

Page

I Introduction   3

II The Everyday World and the World of Science   9

III Time and Space   24

IV Some Contemporary Problems in Understanding Physics   32

V Patterns of Life   37

VI Objections to an Isomorphic Interpretation of the Body-Mind Relationship   48

VII The Physical Basis of Memory and Thought   54

VIII A Preliminary Note on Psychic Phenomena   59

IX The Significance of Mysticism   62

X Psychology and Mysticism   68

XI The Evidence of Mystics   73

XII Aesthetics   81

XIII 'Nature Mysticism' and Primitive Thought   91

XIV Conclusions   94

XV A Note on some of the Basic Concepts of Indian Thought and their Relationship to the theme of this Essay   102

ix

Part II   Page

XVI	Introduction	113
XVII	The Nature of Psycho-Analysis	115
XVIII	Psycho-Analytical Theory	120
XIX	The Super-Ego	126
XX	The 'Authoritarian' and 'Normal' Minds	138
XXI	Some Aspects of Ethics	149
XXII	Ethics and Society	157
XXIII	The Comparison of Societies	169
XXIV	The Aims of Society	173
XXV	Religion and Society	181
XXVI	The Relationship to Christianity	188
XXVII	Some Further Comments and Speculations on Psychic Phenomena	193
XXVIII	Conclusions	200
	Bibliography	204

PART I

I

Introduction

SINCE the time of Descartes probably the most fundamental problem of philosophy, and indeed of Western thought, has been the relationship of the world around us to our experience of it. The countless efforts which have been made to bridge the gap that seems to yawn between them have concentrated above all on the body-mind relationship, to which no generally acceptable solution appears yet to have been recognized. But recently the very formulation of the problem has been questioned. In particular, work by physiologists and psychologists has suggested that the dichotomy is itself suspect, for they have shown that the world is not to be thought of as completely independent of experience, but rather that, in a sense, we each create our own world; that we have to learn to see the world as we do. I shall have occasion to discuss this more fully later, but it is apparent when we think about it that the separation of the world from our experience of it, while it undoubtedly has a wide range of validity, can hardly be fully adequate, if only because we can have no knowledge of the world save by way of our experiences. It would seem, in other words, that the problem might be recast by saying that what is being sought is a system of concepts into which all our experiences will fit.

3

There can, of course, be no question of just slough-
ing off our present system and looking for another: it
is far too deeply integrated into our lives and thoughts
and the very language that we use. Nor has the everyday interpretation of our experiences very much
wrong with it; by and large the world around us
behaves as we expect it to.

But now and then something happens which makes
us pause, for there are quite substantial fields which
find almost no coherent place within our system of
thought. Psychic phenomena are perhaps the most
obvious example. The evidence for their occurrence
seems too strong to doubt, yet they just don't seem to
fit into our ordinary interpretation of the world.
There are other problems, too. What for instance is
the place of aesthetics and religion in our conceptual
system? Is there a God and what do we mean by the
term? And, in some ways of most immediate importance of all, what of the world of moral values?
Whence do they derive their validity? Even in such
specialized fields as microphysics, cosmology and
neurophysiology, the conceptual system seems at times
to be inadequate.

These are very diverse subjects and it would perhaps be surprising to find any link between them. But
that there is such a link it is the aim of this book to
show. It has been known under diverse names and
often under each of these names other attributes have
been associated; and when these other attributes have
been found unnecessary and erroneous or otherwise
explicable, the whole has been discarded.

Thus in philosophy such terms were 'substance', 'essence' and 'being'. These formed an essential part of the conceptual apparatus of philosophy until the early years of this century, when analysis began to come into fashion. Metaphysics had itself tended to become obscure and remote from experience, and, as the intellectual climate changed, many of its ideas tended to lose such intelligibility as they had. Thus 'metaphysics' became a pejorative term and concepts such as substance, being in part meaningless or fallacious, in part obscure and in part perhaps not susceptible of analysis at all, were rejected. They were not, I believe, susceptible of complete analysis because analytical philosophy, being concerned primarily with analysing the meaning of words, naturally concentrates on making clear the differences and distinctions between them. Likewise the words themselves, having grown up in ordinary usage from time immemorial are also concerned to communicate that which is different in experiences. Thus anything common to all words and all experience does not call for, nor indeed is it susceptible of communication or analysis.

Yet that some such idea of substance, being, or God should be implicit in our language and our whole conceptual system, is not, perhaps, surprising, when one thinks that they have both evolved over many thousands of years, during which some sort of belief in deity has been but rarely questioned. Indeed, the problems with which I shall be concerned arise from the disjunction of this implicit conception of the universe, with our everyday explicit ideas deriving from our materialistic view of the world which has no place for such a concept.

Likewise, as I shall attempt to show in more detail presently, the physical sciences, since they are primarily concerned with measurements and with correlating behaviour and formal relationships, and not with what it is that behaves and is the subject of these relationships (if anything), discarded the idea of 'aether'.

Within their limits both science and analytical philosophy have enormously increased and clarified our understanding; but the existence of these limits has not itself been fully appreciated. Thus it has been but a small step thence to denying that anything falls outside them. Accordingly as understanding of the physical world increased and as more and more of the claims of religion, and in particular, of the characteristics attributed to God, became untenable or explicable in terms of the processes of psychology, religion tended to be met with hostility or indifference and the very existence of God came to be widely doubted.

Yet just to discard such concepts as God, substance, Brahman, Tao, or the Ground of the Universe—concepts which have played such a profound rôle both in eastern and in western thought—must cause a few misgivings. Is it not possible that there is some element common to all these which might retain its validity and which might provide some aid in our understanding of the universe? The physical, biological and social sciences and psychology have provided us with insights which are far too well established to do other than accept. Yet in what follows I shall attempt to show that there is one element which is lacking and thus prevents us from fully comprehending what they say. Since God, substance, essence, Brahman, Tao, aether are all words which carry a vast range of implications and overtones, as well as being emotionally evocative, I shall attempt to use as completely neutral a term as I could find—'medium'.

To explain at this point what I mean by 'medium' would involve the use of words which would be misleading or obscure. Accordingly, in the following pages, having first attempted to establish some basis for its use, I treat the existence of the medium almost as an hypothesis in each field to which I turn. Though this approach tends to make the book discursive, in so far as I am successful in my aim, two results will follow. First, the term itself will gradually take on significance for the reader as each subject is explored; and secondly, many of the most important problems which face contemporary thinkers will, I trust, find at any rate a pointer to their solution. Thus what I shall be concerned to do is to point to and to trace the implications of an element which, I believe, is inherent in our whole conceptual system and language but which has been disregarded and disowned in recent years.

The picture which, in so many different fields, I quickly sketch, forms a unitary and integrated conceptual system which may or may not be wholly adequate but which cannot, I believe, in its broad outlines be refuted. Nevertheless the extent to which these two brief essays are successful cannot be measured so much by the answers they provide as by the new lines of thought which may be opened up to those who read them.

II

The Everyday World and the World of Science

ONE of the most obscure and confused parts of contemporary thought lies in our ideas about our everyday perception of the world around us. Here common sense, science and philosophy have become bafflingly intermingled; and since the implications of this tangle spread so far, uncertainty and doubt stemming from this point are to be found undermining and weakening many and diverse parts of knowledge.

I am not concerned in this book to examine in detail the problems and confusions which are found here, nor is my concern to make a specific contribution to their solution. Instead, I want to reach a position from which I can argue from everyday experiences and everyday language, in favour of a conclusion which is unlikely to find easy acceptance, but which, if accepted, has very far reaching implications. Nevertheless some of these problems and confusions will bedevil every argument I wish to use unless I lay them first. Accordingly I shall have to devote most of this preliminary chapter to an attempt to cut a way through this confusing thicket.

The apparently simple act of perception at once becomes complicated when we consider what happens when we suffer illusion. If I look at a stick half-immersed in water it appears to me to be bent, yet all my other experiences convince me that it is in fact still straight. It is convenient to distinguish my perception of the stick from the actual stick, and so the bent appearance is referred to by philosophers as a 'sense-datum'.

It is not, however, possible to tell just from the appearance of the object (as distinct from our knowledge of its surroundings and our past experience of its behaviour) whether the appearance is veridical or illusory. Thus the term sense-datum is extended to cover cases where there is no illusion. We may see a mirage or, looking at a circle obliquely, see an ellipse; cool water may seem warm after we have been holding ice; white objects may appear red in a red light; in all these cases what we actually experience we call a sense-datum, irrespective of whether the experience on its own is misleading or is not.

In this way we are at once able to use different terms to distinguish the appearance of the object from the object itself. But needless to say, to adopt the term 'sense-datum', while it may provide an unambiguous convention, in no way changes the empirical facts of experience.

Some philosophers, it is true, have suggested that sense-data exist without necessarily being experienced; and they have maintained that there is meaning in sentences like 'the green sense-datum I am experiencing is blue'. But these philosophers are still talking about, or are purporting to talk about, ordinary everyday experiences. The differences between the two usages are solely differences of language, and, since the second usage blurs the distinction between the appearance of objects and the objects themselves by giving to sense-data the properties of objects, the value of the distinction is at once lost.

To speak of 'objects themselves' does, of course, itself raise questions, for all we know of objects must derive from our experiences of them. But our experiences so organize and formulate themselves, that the distinction between objects and sense-data is not only valid and useful, but is, indeed, necessary.

Some philosophers have, however, doubted this. The Phenomenalists appreciate that our idea of the physical world is built up in our minds from sense-data. But some of them have put their complete trust in sense-data and have regarded statements about objects which give rise to them as unwarranted assertions about metaphysical entities. For, as they point out, any evidence we can put forward for the existence of objects can only be by way of yet more sense-data.

The Phenomenalist, of course, sees what we see; the empirical facts of observation and of science are known equally to both of us. The difference between us lies not in experience but in language.[1] The virtue of speaking in terms of sense-data is claimed to be that in

[1]Professor Ayer, who is probably the most important and certainly one of the most lucid exponents of the doctrine, himself says '. . . it must be made clear that what the statement that material things consist of sense-data must be understood to designate is not a factual but a linguistic relationship'. (*The Foundations of Empirical Knowledge*, p. 232.)

doing so we are less liable to error in that we speak solely in terms of what is or could be experienced by us. The language (though in practice so cumbersome as to be unusable) would in theory be more precise and would bring in no unwarranted metaphysical overtones.

This belief in the systematically misleading nature of everyday language to-day finds ever declining support among philosophers. Professor Ayer, himself, appears to have modified his views, for he has suggested that '. . . the solution of the "problem of perception" may be to treat our beliefs about physical objects as constituting a theory, the function of which is to explain the course of our sensory experiences.'[1]

Our everyday beliefs about physical objects are not, of course, a theory in any ordinary sense of the word; in particular, such objects must be presupposed by any language, including the language advocated by Phenomenalists. For, in so far as language is concerned with communication, so far must it be concerned with experiences common to those that speak it. Thus in so far as we wish for a language which limits itself to the description of the actual sense-data of the person who speaks it, so far, by definition, are we limiting it to a language describing his private experiences. We are thus putting its subject matter outside the experience of anyone else, and so outside the possibility of communication; thereby we are putting it outside the very idea of language itself. Phenomenalism, which aimed by providing a new language

[1] *Proc. Aristotelian Soc.* Vol. XLVII, 1946–7.

to lend precision to communication, ended by denying its very possibility. Everyday language may, of course, at times be misused or misleading, but it has the enormous advantages of being reasonably accurate and easy to use; and of permitting communication between one person and another.

A second attack, this time upon the everyday view of what the world is like, has come from another flank. It is less subtle, but has perhaps been presented with more energy. It is the attack based on the evidence of science. The physicist, discovering that many things when examined in minute detail have unsuspected properties—for example that the atomic structure of a metal may warrant his saying that it is made up mainly of space—may then argue that the metal is not really solid, and from this it is but a small step to saying that everyday language is misleading. This contention, apparently supported by the inexhaustible factual paraphernalia of the scientist, is capable of bedevilling a number of issues. But it is, of course, fallacious.

The difficulty is that like is not being compared with like. There is no means of giving an everyday account of the microscopic nature of a watch, for it is not an everyday experience; but the scientist can give an account of the microphysical organization of the metal of which it is made. Obviously the two topics are not the same—they differ entirely in scale. Moreover, if I say that the watch is solid and fulfil the necessary logical conditions, there can be no controverting me on that; it is a convention which I am using correctly. Similarly, the scientist will be using a scientific convention quite correctly. But whereas I am talking about a watch, he is talking about the structure of metal. The two accounts are not in this case dealing with the same entity.

If they were in fact to deal with the same entity, namely the watch, there could not be even an apparent conflict. The everyday account of a watch deals with the look, the feel, the use of it, and the way it works; the scientific account, if there were one based on the same entity and using the same scale, would concern itself with the shape, dimensions, mechanisms and properties of the watch. These accounts either overlap or deal with different aspects. Neither contradicts the other nor conflicts with it.

The Phenomenalists aimed to provide an account of the world that was more precise than the everyday account and had none of its metaphysical overtones. The supporters of the scientific attack on the everyday world are perhaps less sure what, if anything, could be used to replace the ordinary account. But what sort of knowledge of the physical world do our ordinary sense-experiences in fact provide? Since it is reasonable to regard the everyday experience as being conditioned and transmitted by the physical mechanisms of sense-perception, let us consider very briefly how those mechanisms operate.

Physical studies of the brain and nervous system have revealed its quite staggering complexity. There are more than 10,000 million nerve cells (or neuron(e)s) in the brain, each connected with others by a large number of fibres which form an interlacing network. These fibres, which can propagate signals extremely rapidly, ensure that the activity of one neurone contributes to the excitation, directly or indirectly, of perhaps hundreds of thousands of other neurones. This activity of the cell, which apparently consists of a momentary escape of some molecules through a sudden change in its surface, produces rapid changes in electrical potential, which, though very small, can be observed. As Professor Adrian says 'We can be reasonably certain that the signals which go to the brain from these different sense-organs are all alike, that they are all the trains of brief nerve-impulses, varying in frequency in each fibre with the intensity of the stimulus, but varying in no other way.'[1]

There are some 100 million separate end-organs on the sensory surface of the retina of the eye, and each optic nerve contains over half a million fibres. These provide the structural basis for the transmission of the information which is conveyed to the visual cortex. Here a pattern corresponding more or less with the pattern of sensory stimulation, is projected. Within the cortex are five projection areas, of which the visual area is one, linked to other parts of the nervous system. It seems probable that the cortex is the physical seat of consciousness. I shall so regard it in what follows, but if it should in the future be found that evidence points to other parts of the brain, this would not upset the principles of my argument.

[1] *The Physical Background of Perception*, p. 21.

Between the sensory organs and the cerebral cortex the signals are, as we have seen, in the form of a coded pattern, of which the constituent events are quite unlike the events making up the original external stimulus, and the events in the sense-organs are different again. Only the resulting events forming the spatio-temporal patterns in the cortex are necessary for the sense-experiences to occur, for, though they are usually generated by stimulation of the sense-organs, they can also be caused by local stimulation of the cortex itself, or of the connexions between the sense-organs and the cortex.

In other words, it would seem that the counterparts of mental events are patterns of physical events in the brain which are causally related by long and complex chains of physical events to patterns of physical events in the outside world.[1] In the case of sight, for example, the response is to the pattern and frequency of electro-magnetic waves. Thus the patterns which are relayed to the cortex are of the same form as the relevant patterns of physical relationships in the outside world.[2]

We have, then, an account provided by science of the events which occur when, for instance, I see a stone.

[1]Professor Adrian concisely describes the physical bases of perception when he says: 'as far as the brain is concerned the function of the sense-organs, or receptors, is to construct in it a map of certain physical events occurring at the surface of the body so as to show what is taking place in the world outside us.'

[2]All our knowledge of these patterns is, of course, dependent upon our sense-experiences, but as part of the subject matter of physics—the scientific study of the formal structure of the physical world—it is independent of any particular sense-experiences.

This account can be summarized briefly and crudely as follows: electro-magnetic waves strike the stone and those frequencies which give rise to our sensations of brownness are reflected and strike our eyes. There, various physical and chemical events take place and issue in trains of impulses along the enormous numbers of fibres leading to the brain. These impulses are, as I have noted, of one form only, each impulse being of an 'all or nothing' type. Finally, in the cortex, which is almost certainly the seat of consciousness, these impulses apparently 'project' a pattern of electrical events which bears a one-to-one relationship to the pattern formed by the electro-magnetic waves falling upon the retina.

A similar account can be provided of the patterns of sound which we hear. For instance, the word, 'black' is in the physical world a pattern of vibrations in the air. These vibrations cause the basilar membrane in the cochlea of the ear to vibrate; the frequency of the waves determines the position of most intense vibration. The associated nerve fibres are excited and pass messages to the auditory area of the cortex. Since different parts of the cortex are linked to corresponding parts of the basilar membrane (of which the different parts vibrate according to the frequency of the impinging waves) the pattern is relayed more or less unchanged. This pattern thus apparently occurs in the air, in the basilar membrane, in the cortex, and in the consciousness.

Plainly, however, there is more to what we see and hear than the form or pattern. The sound, for instance, necessarily has its pitch, and what we see necessarily has its colour. There is every reason to assume that these secondary qualities also are physically stimulated, though the exact processes involved in the physical basis of colour discrimination are not yet clear.

Forms or patterns can be described in terms of physical relationships, and thus are susceptible of causal scientific explanation, but colour or sounds, though associated with certain physical events in the brain, are qualities, and are thus in their nature outside the scope of science; for in the physical sciences the appearance of objects has come to be more and more disregarded and the emphasis has shifted to the classification of these forms or patterns—of the regularities in behaviour of the physical world.[1] If we ask what an electric current is, we are provided with an account of

[1]This point is brought out by Professor Hayek in his book *The Counter Revolution in Science*. As he says, science 'begins with the realization that things which appear to us the same do not always behave in the same manner, and that things which appear different to us sometimes prove in all other respects to behave in the same way; and it proceeds from this experience to substitute for the classification of events which our senses provide a new one which groups together not what appears alike, but what proves to behave in the same manner in similar circumstances'.

In a sense, of course, it is the behaviour itself which is classified and grouped together by science, and not 'what behaves'. As Dr. Toulmin in his book *The Philosophy of Science* says . . . 'physicists seek the form of given regularities'.

This emphasis on form is echoed by Professor Schrödinger in his little book, *Science and Humanism* where, in a section entitled 'Form, not Substance the fundamental concept' he says 'The *new* idea is that what is permanent in these ultimate particles or small aggregates is their shape and organization'.

its behaviour; we may press the matter and be told that it is a stream of electrons surging along a wire. If we then ask what an electron is, we are again provided with an account of observations and measurements, and of inferences from these. But all the time it is its behaviour we are being told about: and what else could we be told about? All that science can say about an atom is to give an account of certain regularities or relationships which, though sometimes extremely complex, have such unity that we can best regard them as the behaviour of an entity which we call an atom.

Thus when we take some common piece of matter—say a stone—and speak of its being made up of molecules and atoms and electrons and so on, we should strictly think of these as different levels in a hierarchy of relationships. There may be excellent justification for speaking of such units in the hierarchy as if they were entities: indeed, their behaviour may be so consistently that of entities and the use of this term so closely analogous to our idea of the stone itself as an entity, that an attempt to criticize the usage would be quite unwarranted. But so far as physics is concerned, it is only their behaviour which is of significance.

Two conclusions can be immediately drawn from this short account. The first is the general one that our ordinary sense-experiences of the world around us depend upon mechanisms which relay solely the forms and patterns of the behaviour which constitutes the physical world. The physical sciences are concerned with the study of these forms and patterns. The same formal relationships thus apparently occur in the brain, in the retina and in the outside world (and are causally related to each other) as appear in consciousness. The second conclusion is a negative one—namely that the relationship between the observable activities in brain cells and the ordinary events of consciousness remain obscure. This, of course, is the age-old difficulty of the body-mind relationship, which is one of the most fundamental of contemporary problems.

Certain implications of everyday language and experience can however be of assistance in dealing with this problem. As we have seen, from consideration of any one sense-datum we would have no reason at all to distinguish the sense-datum itself from what gave rise to it, but we so relate sense-data and our inferences from them that our language is framed mainly in terms not of sense-data but of the physical world. Thus when we speak of a book-case, we speak not only of our immediate sense-data, but also of our conception of the book-case, as built up from our past sense-data and the relationships between them. Further, our ordinary language merges through into the language of science. But, as our ordinary experience tells us, and more advanced knowledge of science confirms, what we know of the book-case depends on its interactions with its environment—to see it, light must shine on it and be reflected from it to our eyes, for instance. But we don't assume that those interactions *are themselves* the book-case. Our everyday language and experience clearly imply that these interactions, this behaviour of the physical world, these relationships, do not exist in abstraction: there must be some-

thing which is their subject—something which inter-
acts, behaves or is related: and this cannot of course
be yet other relationships.

We can bring this point out by means of a simple
diagram. Let us take a very simple case where we have
six relationships—*a* to *f*, which we may show dia-
grammatically thus:

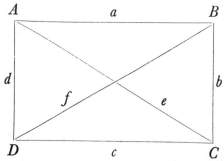

But relationships or behaviour cannot just exist in
abstract: *a*, *b*, *c*, *d*, *e* and *f* are relationships between
A, *B*, *C* and *D*. All we may know of *A* is that it is related to *B*, *C* and *D* by *a*, *e* and *d*, but that in no way
means that *A*, *B*, *C* and *D* *are* these relationships, for
manifestly they are not.

If, then, we are to speak of that which behaves—of
the subject of this behaviour—it would seem that,
since ordinary physical objects are interpenetrated by,
for example electro-magnetic waves and various fields,
all of which are as much manifestations of the subject's behaviour as the objects themselves, we are
driven to think in terms of that which behaves as itself
being all pervasive and of the various physical phenomena as being modes of its behaviour, some being

transient and some being standing patterns. It would appear, in short, that ordinary language and experience imply the existence of some sort of subject of this behaviour—of some sort of medium which manifests the behaviour which itself both constitutes and is relayed by our sense-mechanisms, and forms the subject matter of the physical sciences.

But if indeed everyday language does imply such a medium, why should we accept the implications of everyday language? That of course is the natural reaction, but it is not an appropriate one. For, on the contrary, it rests with an objector to show that everyday language is in some demonstrable way misleading in this respect. But I am suggesting that all our knowledge of the physical world is knowledge of behaviour of a medium; and it is not clear how, empirically, the existence of the medium can be disproved—certainly no experimental means could be devised to disprove its existence; nor could investigations into its behaviour have any relevance to the question of its existence. An attack must presumably be launched along the lines that the postulation of such a medium is unnecessary and unwarranted.

Arguments deriving support from the usage of words are very unlikely to convince anyone, and if I am going to make out a case for the existence of such a medium, or, at least for the value of postulating it, I shall have to provide arguments and evidence a good deal stronger than these.

I shall, therefore, postulate the existence of a non-physical medium and in the following pages I shall attempt to do three related things. The first will be to show that at least this is a device which enables me not only to provide a reasonable and coherent synthesis of a number of fields of knowledge and experience, but also enables me to provide a reasonable basis for solving some of the most puzzling problems in contemporary thought. The second will be to provide certain positive evidence in favour of the existence of such a medium. And the third will be to build up a full and significant meaning for the concept.[1]

Now of the problems I shall have to consider, two of the most puzzling and fundamental are time and space. Accordingly let us first to these turn our attention.

[1]It may, of course, be objected that this 'medium' is just an attempt to reintroduce into the scheme of things the long-discredited 'substance'. But as I explained in the Introduction, I have purposely avoided the term 'substance' because of its multiplicity of meanings, most of which have been shown to be demonstrably false, having been introduced as a misconceived extension of the everyday use of the word and endowed by analogy with the properties of the world around us. It may, however, be further objected that the 'medium' postulated here is just such an analogy, and is open to the same objections. But the 'medium' as here conceived has no physical properties whatever over and above the properties which form the subject matter of science.

III

Time and Space[1]

THE concept of time has provided an important stumbling block to philosophers, theologians, and scientists. When St. Augustine made his famous observation[2] he might have been expressing a contemporary view.

Ultimately, all our knowledge of the world rests upon our own personal experiences and we must accordingly try to discern what experiences we have which relate to time. Obviously we are immediately aware of the order of events we experience. Closely related to this is our awareness of change—change as sunshine follows shadow, as day follows night, winter follows summer, age follows youth.

[1]Since these views were formulated and this chapter drafted, the fifteenth edition of Einstein's *Relativity* has come to hand. In the Preface he added a note to this edition which reads as follows: 'In this edition I have added, as a fifth appendix, a presentation of my views on the problem of space in general and on the gradual modification of our ideas on space resulting from the influence of the relativistic view-point. I wished to show that space-time is not necessarily something to which one can ascribe a separate existence, independently of the actual objects of physical reality. Physical objects are not *in space*, but these objects are *spatially extended*. In this way the concept "empty space" loses its meaning.' This is the interpretation which I have put forward independently in this chapter.

[2]'Quid est ergo tempus? Si nemo a me quaerat, scio; si quaerenti explicare velim, nescio!'—'What is time? If no one asks me, I know; if I want to explain it to an inquirer, I don't know!'

We are directly aware of change—acutely so in all the bustle of city life where every minute presses, but less so in the country. In the city we pay attention to the hours and minutes, and the seasons and years slip by less markedly. In the country it is the seasons and years, life and death, sowing and harvest that are the significant markers of time. By choosing the years and the days as our basic units of time, and their sub-divisions of the hours, minutes and seconds, we have a measure of rate of change. These provide our basic clocks. The daily journeys of the sun round the sky, like the movements of the hands of a man-made clock, are changes in space. By taking some part or multiple of such changes, we can measure all other changes.

Away from any change which can act as a clock, however, we rapidly lose all idea of what time has passed. When we wait even a few minutes for some event—the arrival of a friend or the boiling of a kettle —time seems to tarry. In the midst of gaiety and rapid change, as at a party, we look in dismay at our watches to see how rapidly the time has fled. If we fall asleep in our chairs in the afternoon, two minutes or two hours seem indistinguishable.

If, then, we concentrate, can we distinguish the passage of time as such? Here each person must speak for himself, but, apart from experiencing any change which gives an indication of the passage of time—even if such change be only one's consciousness of one's own heart beats, there seems to be complete failure to experience anything which could be considered to be the passage of time.

That time is a rather sophisticated elaboration of change is borne out by what we know of the earliest ideas of time. Whitrow says 'it seems that for primitive people time consisted of disconnected fragments; there was no concept of time as a whole, only of convenient fractions of time, e.g., so many moons.' Indeed, the hour of fixed length was introduced only in the fourteenth century. Time itself would thus seem to have no physical reality and to be an abstraction by our own minds from our experience of change. Nothing in our direct personal experiences appears to falsify this conclusion, but it obviously needs to be reconciled with the physicist's understanding of time.[1]

Now time—or rate of change—can be measured in a number of different ways. The way most generally used is, as I have remarked, to take as standard the time taken to cover a certain distance in space. This applies to the earth's annual journey round the sun, the daily rotation of the earth, or the moving of the hands of a clock. But there are, of course, other ways —for instance the decay of electric charge in a condenser, the decay of heat from a certain body or the break down of radio-active material. This last way is in fact used by geologists as a means for dating rocks.

The measurement of time may be considered from three aspects. First it must be decided what type of sequence of change is to be chosen—whether, for

[1]The following paragraphs owe much to the published works of Professor Dingle. In particular—*Through Science to Philosophy*, Oxford 1937.

instance, changes in space of a moving body, or changes in heat in a cooling body. Secondly, the particular sequence must be selected—whether the moving body be the hand of a particular clock or the rotation of a binary star. Thirdly, there is the standard of measurement to be chosen—in the case of the rotating earth, one rotation might be defined by reference to the stars or the sun or the moon. Now we are apparently entirely free to choose under each of these headings whichever is the most convenient to us in correlating experience.

It was the theory of Relativity that revealed our freedom to choose any standard by which to define equal intervals of space, and to choose any sequence of spatial positions which we wish to be measured to define equal time intervals; but the freedom to choose different kinds of sequence of events, e.g., movements in space or decay of heat, was not explicitly shown.

It has always been customary, of course, to make the measure of time proportional to the measure of space, and since we now know the standard of space measurement is ultimately a matter of choice, equal time intervals must also ultimately be a matter of choice too. Accordingly the common equation of time with space is valid only so long as we retain the convention of measuring time in terms of space. If we had chosen to measure time in terms of temperature, time would be equated not to space but to temperature.

Thus when we measure the change in position of a certain object in a certain time, we measure that time in terms of the change of position of another, standard, object (a clock hand or the earth); we are thus measuring a change of position in space in terms of another change of position in space—in other words, we retain change, as of course we must, but we eliminate time other than as a concept.

If I have interpreted this aspect of the theory of Relativity correctly, all we do when we 'measure time' is to compare one change with other changes, and time becomes a fiction—a most valuable, and for everyday purposes obviously indispensable fiction, but a fiction none the less.

If, then, there is any validity in this interpretation of time as only an abstraction from our experiences of change, we must concentrate our attention rather more closely on change. It does not occur in isolated instances but is a part of a great system interacting one part with another, and of this system we ourselves form an integral part. Change in our everyday experience is, of course, continuous and consequently time is, too.

The changes of which we are conscious originate either in our minds or in the physical world around us, and even where these changes originate in our minds, I hope to show that they have physical counterparts: indeed, that physical events can be regarded as the forms of 'mental' events. All these changes, as I have said, are part of the great system of change which constitutes the physical world. Since 'ex hypothesi' this system of change is the change or behaviour of an underlying medium, and since, as I have suggested, the concept of time derives from such changes in the medium, we have no reason to assume that it applies to the medium itself.[1]

By assuming time to be a concept derived from changes in the medium, some of the objections to regarding time either as finite or infinite are substantially lessened, for on this basis the medium does not itself exist in time: time does not apply to the medium, for it derives from the changes in the medium. Accordingly, whether or not time had a beginning or whether it extends back to infinity depends simply on whether or not there was a first change. If we assume, as seems *prima facie* more reasonable, that there was a first change, then *ex hypothesi* there was no time before it. It is true that the postulation of a first event raises difficulties about its causation. But these need not be insuperable, for, as we shall see more clearly as the argument unfolds, the medium as here conceived is self-motivating.

Similar arguments to those I have been putting forward about time apply to space. With the coming of Relativity it, too, lost many of the properties which have been ascribed to it. The modern physicist no longer believes in absolute space, for, by combining his knowledge of the various geometries which have been developed by mathematicians with his own observations, he has been able to ascribe to space new, non-Euclidean properties which are equally consistent with his observations and yet which allow the laws of nature

[1]Likewise if we say that the path of a whirling handle is circular, that gives us no reason at all for assuming that the handle itself is circular.

to take fundamentally simpler forms. Since, however, all these spaces can be regarded as Euclidean for distances which are small when compared with their radius of curvature, their differences would become discernible only over distances reaching to the more remote parts of the universe.

Like time, space cannot be directly perceived. Time, I suggested, was a mental construction from change. Can anything similar be said of space?

Space is mysterious in that we cannot perceive it, nor any indication of its presence; the absence of space implies the presence of an object, yet if we remove the object there is—nothing. Is space, then, nothing? Clearly it is not a thing.

In Chapter VI we shall quote from Professor J. Z. Young's 'Reith Lectures' a passage which shows how the distinguishing of objects in three dimensions is something which we learn over a considerable period of time as we become aware of them in relation to ourselves and in relation to other objects.

Thus, like time, space is a mental construction, a construction from our awareness of the order, relations and arrangements of things amongst themselves and in relation to us. Without things it is nothing. In other words space, like time, has no physical reality apart from the physical objects from whose spatial relations we abstract the concept of space; this we then mistakenly regard as an entity in its own right.

On this new basis some of the conceptual difficulties about the curvature of space and the idea of a finite universe vanish. Einstein assumed the universe to be finite though unbounded. Since space is the relationship between objects, space can extend no farther than the outermost objects and the outermost extension space must be formed by the relationship between the outermost objects. But however far the outermost objects extend, they might always conceivably extend farther, even to infinity.

Space, in other words, we must regard as a concept derived from the spatial relationships between objects and these I earlier gave grounds for considering as patterns of behaviour of a medium. If, however, the idea of space derives from the behaviour of the medium, then, as we have seen, we have no reason at all to assume that it, any more than time, in any way limits or even applies to the medium itself. Clearly, however, such a non-physical medium, to which neither time nor space apply, underlying all physical events, needs to be reconciled with the findings of contemporary physics. Accordingly, I shall next indicate the place and value of such a concept there.

IV

Some Contemporary Problems in Understanding Physics

THE medium certainly appears to be a fruitful concept when applied to certain outstanding difficulties in contemporary physics.

Lord Samuel in his recently published *Essay in Physics* dealt with certain of these problems. In particular he considered:

(1) The nature of electro-magnetic radiation and the medium for its transmission;

(2) the nature of gravitation and its propagation;

(3) the nature of motion and momentum; and

(4) the nature of the waves and particles that are studied by physics and the relations between them.

To meet the difficulties arising on each of these points he put forward the view 'that energy exists in two states—quiescent and active, and passes easily from one to the other.

'Quiescent energy is conceived as a continuum, and as the sole physical constituent of the universe. All material events are to be accounted for as cases of the activation of quiescent energy.

'Being quiescent it is undifferentiated, and produces no phenomena. It cannot be perceived, or defined, or described, and nothing can be located or timed by reference to it.

32

'It does not follow from this that it is non-existent. Its existence is demonstrated by the emergence and behaviour of active energy. It is one of those un-observables whose reality is inferred from the pheno-mena that have been observed.'[1]

The similarities, so far as physics is concerned, be-tween these views and the views put forward in this book will be readily apparent. As a reading of Lord Samuel's book will show, there seems very little doubt that the introduction of a 'medium' into an account of these phenomena would greatly help us to understand them.

It may be objected that this would involve reintro-ducing an 'aether'. There were, however, two aspects of aether which were not always separated: it was regarded as having certain residual physical pro-perties which could not be absorbed into the main body of physics; and it was regarded as a medium forming the substratum of the phenomena of physics. As the scientific account of the physical world became more complete, the first of these disappeared; and because the exact sciences became more and more able to provide a coherent abstract account using formal relationships alone, the concept of a medium under-going these relationships was found to be unnecessary.

But although the physical properties of aether were, one after another, absorbed into the general body of physics, the idea of the aether as a medium under-going these various forms of behaviour has never been disproved. (It is not of course in its nature capable of

[1]Op. cit., pp. 46–47.

disproof.) It has been discarded by physics because such a medium must, as we have indicated, be strictly extra-scientific and non-physical and as such, unnecessary in describing in mathematical terms the formal relationships it undergoes. The difficulty of understanding these phenomena (as distinct from describing them in mathematical terms) could, however, as Lord Samuel has shown by reference to his concept of quiescent energy, be greatly eased by the introduction of a medium into the account.

A branch of physics where the acceptance of a medium would probably be of particular help in explaining a number of very important and pressing problems is in quantum mechanics. Here the situation has been reached that if one equates existence and observability, then the basic units of matter have no continuity of existence; alternatively we may say that they have periods of change in which they are unobservable, and then reappear in a different form which cannot be related causally to any previous state. We thus apparently have to interpret these phenomena either as evidence of discontinuous existence or of the incomplete causal dependence of observable facts.

To meet this situation has been devised what Professor Schrödinger describes as 'The Makeshift of Wave Mechanics'. 'It amounts to this: we do give a complete description, continuous in space and time without leaving any gaps, conforming to the classical ideal —a description of *something*. But we do not claim that this "something" is the observed or observable facts;

and still less do we claim that we thus describe what nature (matter, radiation, etc.) really *is*. In fact we use this picture (the so-called wave picture) in full knowledge that it is *neither*.

'There is no gap in this picture of wave mechanics, also no gap as regards *causation*.' But 'the information we get as regards the causal dependence of observable facts is incomplete. (The cloven hoof must show up somewhere!)'[1]

This theory did not satisfy its originator, Max Planck, nor did it satisfy Einstein, any more than it satisfies Professor Schrödinger and many others. For instance, Planck wrote 'I firmly believe, in company with most physicists, that the quantum hypothesis will eventually find its exact expression in certain equations which will be a more exact formulation of the law of causality.'[2] Professor Einstein on a number of occasions expressed similar views.

If, however, these phenomena were to be regarded simply as the behaviour of a medium, the horror with which the idea of intermittent existence is viewed would presumably vanish. There would at such moments simply be no observable behaviour of the medium taking place. So far as physics is concerned— with its subject matter limited to the behaviour of the medium—these units would cease to exist. But since the existence of the non-physical medium is not intermittent that would present no problem. Further, there would be a strong presumption that the intuition of

[1] *Science and Humanism*, pp. 40–1. C.U.P. 1951.
[2] *Where is Science Going?* p. 143. Allen & Unwin, 1933.

both Planck and Einstein that an 'exact formulation of the law of causality' should be possible, was correct, even though all the behaviour of the 'medium' might not prove in practice, to be observable.

There are also other parts of physics where the idea of a medium might prove significant; in cosmology and, in particular, in considering the theories of continuous creation, and in low temperature physics, for instance.

Clearly, then, the introduction into physics of the idea of a non-physical medium of the nature here suggested bears a *prima facie* possibility of being of value, and can certainly not reasonably be rejected out of hand. So far as physics is concerned, it can at most be regarded as unnecessary.

On the other hand, although such a non-physical medium might greatly help in the exposition of physics, it is strictly irrelevant to the experimental side of physics, and accordingly, in its nature, no experimental evidence of physics could prove or disprove its existence.

Now microphysics is concerned with the basic units of all matter, whether non-living or living, and no clear-cut dividing line can be drawn between them. In the next chapter I shall indicate how, by introducing the idea of the medium, the problems of the relationships between life and matter and body and mind find a solution within our interpretation. This, however, will require some consideration of the nature of the physical systems which are involved.

V

Patterns of Life[1]

LIVING organisms take innumerable forms, varying from a single cell to the enormous complexity of a multi-cellular organism. A human being has rather more than 100,000 (English) billion cells; each cell has about 10,000 million atoms and is the seat of a multiplicity of complex chemical and physical processes. Not only the forms but the processes of life are unique. The organism maintains itself in its high state of organization by a continuous interchange of materials and energy with the outside world; it can show spontaneous activity and react to stimuli; each organism is reproduced by parent organisms of the same form; each individual develops and dies; forms change through geological time; each is extremely closely adapted to its environment; each is an extremely complex and highly organized system.

Within such a system each part depends not only on conditions within itself but also on the conditions within the whole, while the whole exhibits properties which are not to be found in its isolated parts. No fundamental difference is to be found in an individual

[1]Much of what is said in this chapter applies to all living organisms, but since in no way can it be comprehensive, I have not attempted to deal specifically with plants. The chapter owes much to *Problems of Life* by L. von Bertalanffy. Watts, 1952.

phenomenon between living and non-living, for even extremely complex processes such as, for instance, nerve action have been largely explained in terms of physics and chemistry. It is in the organization and wholeness of the organism that the characteristics of life are to be found. The emphasis on organization is accentuated when it is appreciated that the organism is constantly changing its own components, for these are perpetually breaking down and being renewed; at the same time it is an active system able to regulate itself in response to disturbances.

Organisms are built up from the basic units of all matter—the atoms. Atoms themselves are composed of electrons, protons and other units which partake partly of the characteristics of waves and partly of particles. Atoms are however much more definite entities than these and exhibit quite distinct properties. They in turn form molecules and these likewise have characteristics quite different from those of the atoms of which they are composed. Water has very different properties from those of the hydrogen and oxygen atoms of which it is formed, yet it could have none of these properties but for them. Inorganic molecules are in general relatively simple compared with organic molecules, some of which are of enormous complexity.

When such molecules combine into high-molecular organic compounds new forces, or secondary valences, appear which are the forces of cohesion of solid bodies. These compounds likewise exhibit properties which are different from those of the molecules which make them up. With the increase of complexity there occurs an indefiniteness in structure. For example, the formula for a substance such as cellulose cannot be stated precisely but only in statistical form. The units of which such a substance is composed are thus arranged in continuous hierarchy of levels and at each structural level the degree of indefiniteness or freedom increases.

Beyond these compounds comes the border-land between animate and inanimate in which are found viruses. With a single atom of hydrogen as the unit, water has a weight of 18, the simplest real protein 17,000 and the tobacco-mosaic virus 40·7 million; yet most viruses are so small that they can be made visible only with the aid of powerful electron microscopes. These viruses have the power of reproduction and thus have one of the basic characteristics of life, but they can reproduce only within the tissues of their host. Once again they exhibit properties quite different from those of the units of which they are composed.

Comparable in many respects to viruses are the basic units of heredity, the genes, which are linked together to form rod-like particles or chromosomes. These genes are practically certainly large molecules of incredible complexity containing probably of the order of 1 million atoms. The stability of these molecules is very great, as is evidenced by the number of organisms which have retained essentially the same form for many millions of years. The way in which these units grow is still not definitely known. Like all biological systems they are continuously exchanging material with their environment, and thus are dynamic structures which are not at rest but in a steady state.

Genes are essential units of cells, and viruses are parasites on cells. Cells are the simplest systems capable of autonomous existence and form the basic and dynamic units of all living things. The basic material of which the cell is composed is protoplasm, which is maintained, like other organic substances, by a continuous process of building-up and breaking-down while the whole is in a self-regulating steady state. Once more we see that the cell exhibits properties different from those of the units of which it is composed.

Within an organism cells are organized in hierarchies, and each cell is a member of a number of such hierarchies. Thus, for example, there is a hierarchy deriving from the process of division whereby from one cell are derived other cells in a hierarchy of generations. There are hierarchies of organization according to the grouping of cells in space to form, e.g., organs, which in turn are grouped through several levels to form the organism as a whole. Likewise the physiological processes themselves can be classified in hierarchies, beginning, for instance, with physico-chemical processes within a single cell, and extending in successive levels through simple reflexes to reactions of the body as a whole. These physiological hierarchies of processes by no means correspond with the morphological hierarchies of parts, for morphologically quite unrelated parts co-operate in physiological processes.

All these hierarchies interact with varying degrees of

closeness according to the nature of the organism. In general the higher the organism the more closely integrated are the hierarchies, and yet the more differentiated and less adaptable are its parts. These become specialized to particular functions and thus less able to take over other functions of the organism in time of need. With the increase in integration and at the same time of differentiation goes increasingly centralized control. When there is little or no centralization, it is difficult to distinguish individuals, for although individual cells may die the mass as a whole can live indefinitely. With increasing centralization not only do certain parts become vital to the whole, so that on their death the entire organism dies, but also the interests of the organism increasingly dominate the interests of the parts, so that in extremity parts will be sacrificed to the whole. In any case, the potentialities of each cell are limited in the interests of the organism, and the way in which each develops is determined by its position in the whole.

Yet although development of each cell is subordinated in the interests of the whole, these interests are not to be conceived of as directed towards some future state, but by the actual state of the organism at any given time. Thus in abnormal circumstances such development may lead to biologically pointless results, notably if cells are removed from their place in the organism and thus from its controlling influence, while at the same time being supplied with food.

The amazingly complex development of an organism is apparently controlled in the first instance by the chemical activity of the genes. This takes place through the activity of hormone-like substances by which the various activities in the body are directed and accelerated or retarded. The nature of the basic developmental process, as distinct from its regulation, is not, however, apparently susceptible of explanation in physico-chemical terms.

The development of the organism is characterized by development towards higher levels of order, and if an organism were a closed system, this would be contrary to the second law of thermo-dynamics by which, in a closed system, a decrease of order (or increase in entropy) takes place. However, an organism is not, in fact, a closed but an open system for it is continuously drawing energy from its surroundings. A great many difficulties arise from thinking of an organism as static. Organisms are complex, dynamic, self-motivating and self-regulating open systems. We may compare such a complex system with a very simple open system—a fountain. Here, too, as in an organism, behaviour is clearly strictly causal, and yet, in that it returns to the same position after having been deflected by the wind, its behaviour is in a primitive sense purposive. Where feed-back mechanisms occur as in calculating machines or living organisms, the purposive behaviour becomes much more obvious. It is, of course, complementary to and in no sense in conflict with the causal aspects of their behaviour, and forms one of the fundamental characteristics of living organisms.

A second fundamental characteristic is the way in which the future development of the organism is apparently contained in its earlier form. Many of the difficulties of this conception are simplified by considering the particular form of the development as moulded through the intervention of the genes in a dynamic flow of processes. In this intervention the co-operation of a number of genes to form a particular characteristic is usual.

The gene endowment is inherited, as are variations in it. This, and the constant over-production of offspring are the fundamental features of evolution. No unlimited increase in the number of surviving individuals takes place, and in the struggle for existence a favourable variation in gene-endowment will give an advantage, which will rapidly be extended in successive generations. However, in such delicately harmonized processes as those of a living organism the genic balance is easily upset and thus most mutations will be lethal. Even, however, when they are favourable the genic balance is unlikely to be firmly established again until a number of mutations have taken place. In such circumstances the operation of selection is likely to be particularly effective, and thus a rapid series of changes is likely to take place until another position of stability is found, often considerably removed from the starting point.

Nevertheless, the changes undergone by organisms are by no means fortuitous, for they are limited, apparently, by the variations which are possible in the individual genes, by the possibilities of their development in the genic system as a whole, and by the general laws of biological organization.

Thus although it is highly improbable that the biological world will ever be explicable entirely in physico-chemical terms, for new laws applicable only to biological phenomena are in process of being discovered, nevertheless, it would seem that the two systems cannot be sharply differentiated, and that their laws will ultimately be seen clearly to belong to one unified system.

This system is apparently hierarchical, having at its first level the statistical laws of microphysics; above this are the levels of macrophysical phenomena where statistical variations are smoothed out in the great number of fluctuations; at the biological levels, single processes can be distinguished and explained in terms of physics and chemistry, while different laws, applicable only to biological phenomena apply to organisms as wholes. Finally there are those laws which apply to social groups but can again be stated only statistically. At each level new characteristics appear. These in no way conflict with, but are different from, and cannot be completely explained in terms of, the lower-level units of which each unit is composed. It is at the level of viruses and cells that those characteristics appear which we classify as life. At the higher levels still appear characteristics which we classify as those of mind. Upon these atoms, molecules, viruses, cells and organisms, we look as it were, from the outside. But we, each one of us, are such organisms ourselves.

Can we, then, point to any one thing and say 'this is life'? We can of course point to living things, to cells and their nuclei, for instance, but there is nothing we can point to as 'life'. If indeed we were to look for it, what could we hope to find? We could find further physical objects conceivably, but life is not a physical object. We already know a lot about the nature of living matter: we know for instance that the greater part of a living organism is made up of half a dozen common chemical elements. Life, however, is not that sort of thing at all—it is not a thing. It is, in short, a mode of behaviour. It is the way in which matter behaves under certain circumstances—roughly when it reaches a certain very high degree of complexity and organization.

Matter, however, if we are to regard it as the dead inert stuff of the physical world must nevertheless have some very remarkable properties, if, in certain groupings it starts to live, and indeed, becomes each one of us. There seem no grounds for regarding matter as dead inert stuff when I stub my toe! Clearly the world is as it is and, in general, the main facts are not in dispute in considering the problem of life; our difficulties are, in short, conceptual. They arise, at any rate in part, because, when we work our way down the hierarchy of organization from the most complex towards its simpler units, we find that the simple units are not only non-living, but also that they are identical with units which go to make up the ordinary physical world around us. It is, in other words, in the complexity of organization of organisms that the main secret of life seems to lie.

I have, however, earlier given grounds for regarding matter as patterns of behaviour: accordingly the secret of life would more properly be regarded as lying in the complexity of organization of behaviour, and, of course, on the hypothesis I have put forward, it is the behaviour of a medium, itself non-physical, which is in question.

Once we have the non-physical medium, then, our conceptual difficulties begin to lessen for we may look upon those characteristics which we associate with life as characteristics of the behaviour of the medium when its behaviour is organized in certain complex ways.

Now I have already indicated that the behaviour of open systems can be at the same time both causal and (in the sense we have indicated) purposive, and that there is no necessary conflict between these complementary aspects. A calculating machine may try many different ways in order to solve a problem, yet it is plainly a causal mechanism. Unlike an organism, however, a calculating machine is not conscious. This subjective element forms a great stumbling-block in contemporary thought, and, in its more specialized form, it is, of course, the body-mind problem, which, in many ways, is the most important and fundamental problem facing contemporary thinkers.

Let us then invoke the medium and ascribe to it the property of consciousness when so organized. I can then ascribe to the medium the characteristic of behaving according to certain laws—its causal aspect; furthermore, while remaining strictly causal, it can, as I have indicated, be purposive; and, in so far as the medium is aware of its own behaviour, it is conscious: subjective, purposive and causal thus become three complementary dimensions of an organism and, although I may have a long way to go before I have shown this adequately, the body-mind problem disappears. From one point of view the medium becomes conscious of its own behaviour; from the other the behaviour becomes self-conscious. Either way, however, an isomorphic interpretation of the body-mind relationship is implied. Since certain important objections have been raised to such an interpretation, I must now consider them and show that they do not apply to the views I have put forward here. At the same time I shall hope to make clearer the implications of these views.

VI

Objections to an Isomorphic Interpretation of the Body-Mind Relationship

In considering objections to an isomorphic interpretation of the body-mind relationship I must first make clear that the part played by the perceiver is by no means passive. Professor J. Z. Young in his 'Reith Lectures' illustrates this from cases where people born blind have later received their sight as a result of an operation. He describes what happens thus:

'The patient on opening his eyes for the first time gets little or no enjoyment; indeed, he finds the experience painful. He reports only a spinning mass of lights and colours. He proves to be quite unable to pick out objects by sight, to recognize what they are, or to name them. He has no conception of space with objects in it, although he knows all about objects and their names by touch. "Of course", you will say, "he must take a little time to learn to recognize them by sight." Not a little time, but a very, very long time, in fact, years. His brain has not been trained in the rules of seeing . . . What these people lack is the store of rules in the brain, rules usually learnt by the long years of exploration with the eyes during childhood . . . Contrary to what we might suppose, the eyes and brain do not simply record in a sort of photographic manner

48

the pictures that pass in front of us . . . we have to learn to see the world as we do.'[1]

We have seen that modern neurology has found that any picture falling upon the retina of the eye is projected on to the occipital cortex where the physical counterparts of visual events apparently occur. Nevertheless, it would seem at first sight that the form of the projections is such as to give rise to serious objections to regarding mental and physical events as isomorphic.

The first difficulty is that the projection is inverted; this is not a strong objection, however, as the optical frame of reference must itself be inverted. A much more serious difficulty is that the two right half-retinas are projected upon the striate cortex of the right hemisphere of the brain, whereas the two left half-retinas are projected upon the striate cortex of the left hemisphere of the brain. The gap between the two areas is bridged anatomically by the corpus callosum; but even when this has been surgically divided, we are not aware of any gap in our vision. The problem of how the two sides of the visual field are joined in our consciousness would thus appear to present a major problem.

Let us make an analogy. Let us imagine ourselves in a darkened cinema with a very wide screen on which is projected a picture. One half of the picture is, however, projected on to the right of the screen and one half on to the left, while between there is darkness. Our

[1] pp. 61–6, 'Doubt and Certainty in Science'—the *B.B.C. Reith Lectures*, 1950, published by the O.U.P., 1951.

problem is how the two parts are brought together. We in the cinema, are, of course, conscious of the darkness; but there is no evidence that we are in any way conscious of events in the area of the brain between the projection areas. In other words there is nothing of which we are conscious dividing the areas, and there would thus seem to be no reason to expect to be conscious of some division, unless we are misled by the analogy. This is not to say, of course, that there would not remain the task of co-ordinating the two sides, but this we may assume to be something that we learn. Accordingly this objection to an isomorphic theory is not one which applies to the interpretation of the body-mind relationship which I am here putting forward.

A second apparently major problem which must be met by any isomorphic theory is that, though the retina has an evenly and gently curving surface, the corresponding part of the cortex is very strongly and unevenly folded. Thus, if we think of some observer looking down upon the events in the cortex, this would undoubtedly completely distort any picture which has been relayed from the retina. Here again, however, to think of an observer looking at the cortex is to use a doubtful analogy. According to the theory I am putting forward, the mental and physical events are two aspects of the same event. To put the matter crudely, we may think of the physical event as conscious of itself. The distortion which occurs in the case of an observer in a fixed position separated from a corrugated surface which he is observing is thus eliminated and this objection, too, if made against the theory I am putting forward here, no longer stands.

There are, however, yet other objections to an isomorphic theory of mind. The central part of the retinal image is enlarged some six times in the cortex, and this, it has been suggested, ought, if the isomorphic theory were correct, to cause a corresponding distortion in our consciousness. This, however, is by no means necessarily true.

The events which occur while we are still learning to use our eyes are of greatly varied form. We cannot know when we are little that a particular object or pattern is always the same size, or that the variations which we experience derive from any particular cause; an object may, for instance, be farther away from us; we have to find this out by experience. We must, in short, think not of a geographer drawing a map on a particular projection and scale; rather, he is given maps with no details of the projection and scale and has by experience to find out by correlating his observations what are their characteristics so that he can learn to use them. Once more the objection, at any rate as applied to the theory which I am putting forward, arises from a false analogy.

There is, however, yet another objection to the isomorphic theory which we must consider. This derives from the fact that in looking at some scene, its features are constantly shifting about on the surface of the retina and so in the cortex; we look at one part and then another, sometimes closely, sometimes from a distance, and in no particular order, and yet we manage to build up in our minds a perfectly satis-factory picture of what is before us. Somehow all these constantly shifting views are combined and co-ordinated. Yet what we see at any one moment fills the receptive area of the cortex, and is constantly being replaced by some variation in the scene.

This would seem to be the most complex of the difficulties we have faced and is one to which we can attempt no full answer. Yet the difficulties in the way of an isomorphic theory even here would seem not to be insuperable, and it is a difficulty which must be faced by any attempt to correlate events in the brain with those of the mind.

When we consider all the many different aspects of a landscape which we have seen, only a very few remain in our memory for any length of time. Many vanish almost at once. There is, however, no fixed barrier between the conscious and the subconscious. When we recognize something, we do not bring into full consciousness our recollections, though they are often available if necessary. Instead, they remain below the level of consciousness, but give rise to a sense of familiarity. Something similar must happen in perception. Perhaps the physical patterns which form the counterparts of what we see reverberate in the brain for a few moments; and a few may cause physical changes in the brain which allow them to be reactivated later. The combination and co-ordination involved in these processes, though they must be of enormous complexity, would seem to be mainly pro-cesses of association giving rise to a sense of familiarity.

These processes, complex as they are, do not appear to be different or necessarily more difficult than many accomplished by the brain. There is, at any rate apparently, no good reason to assume that these processes do not occur in the brain. In so far, the point can hardly be considered an objection which applies particularly to an isomorphic theory; and if it were established that mental events do, in fact, occur without physical counterparts in the brain, the interpretation which I am in process of putting forward could much more easily take account of them than any epiphenomenalist[1] argument.

[1]Epiphenomenalism is the doctrine that all mental events are entirely determined by physical events and do not themselves determine anything.

VII

The Physical Basis of Memory and Thought

THIS discussion of the handling of visual information leads me to consider very briefly the physical basis of thought and of memory, and how far our knowledge is compatible with this theory of the body-mind relationship.

One of the basic mental processes is that of recognition and this implies that there is no fixed barrier between the conscious and the subconscious. As I have noted, when we recognize something we do not bring into full consciousness our recollections and compare them with what we see. Instead, having been raised to the subconscious, they give rise to a sense of familiarity which we describe as recognition.

Closely linked with recognition is association. When somebody says 'vase', not only do we recognize the sound of the word but we associate it with a whole range of objects and ideas. We do not have to bring into consciousness images of particular vases, though we could do so if necessary. The sound 'vase', in fact, has a cluster of associations, some close, some distant, which remain in our subconscious and give rise to this sense of familiarity. The word crystallizes and stands for, or means, this penumbra of associations. It is the use of the word which shows its meaning, but in using it meaningfully, its use gives rise to an experience closely akin to the experience of recognition.

54

One of the words immediately associated with the word 'vase' is 'glass'; this has its own group of associations and so its own 'meaning'. Plainly some of the associations of the word 'vase' correspond with those of the word 'glass', but it has other quite different associations. There is, we might say, a most complex multi-dimensional tapestry of associations and meanings in which each word or group of words has many associations, and different combinations of these are subsumed under yet other words which have their own associations, including the words which they subsume. A small part of this tapestry can be brought into consciousness and a somewhat larger part into the subconscious at any one time.

How, then, does this tapestry get woven? Some strands are already woven when we are born, but most are formed by experience. As we learn to organize our sense-experiences, gradually numberless association linkages are formed. The sound 'vase' is perhaps linked to the image of an object by ostensive definition and a firm association is established. Then when we see a vase we tend to think of the sound 'vase' or at any rate it lies fairly close to the level of consciousness. It is, however, only when the sound 'vase' becomes an integral part of the tapestry, and we use it with other words each with their own associations, that we say we know the 'meaning' of the word. Of course, when the tapestry is fairly well integrated (though not necessarily extensive) it becomes unnecessary always to use ostensive definition—the associations of other associated words can become grouped together so that the new word 'means' this set of associations; this must be the case with the word 'unicorn', for instance.

The 'tapestry' must, it would seem, have a physical counterpart. As Eccles says:

'In general, it may be postulated that any thought pattern in the mind has a counterpart in a specific spatio-temporal pattern of neuronal activity . . . Memory of any particular event is dependent on a specific reorganization of neuronal associations . . . in a vast system of neurones widely spread over the cerebral cortex . . . Lashley has convincingly argued that "the activity of literally millions of neurons" is involved in the recall of any memory . . . We may say that the remembered thought appears in the mind as its specific spatio-temporal pattern is being replayed in the cortex.'[1] Later he says:

'. . . the spontaneous electrical activity in the cerebral cortex is explicable by impulses circulating in spatio-temporal patterns in the unimaginably complex neuronal network of the cerebral cortex . . . There are some ten thousand million neurones in the human cerebral cortex . . . and each is a node in the network . . . Each node would be the convergent point of scores of paths and each in turn would project to scores of other nodes.'[2]

Plainly, a prodigious number of patterns is possible, even when we consider the complexity of some of our memories. Further, we might expect, and there is good evidence, that complex memories are groupings of less

[1] *The Neurophysiological Basis of Mind*, p. 266. Oxford, 1953.
[2] Ibid., p. 268.

complex memories and so on in a considerable hierarchy.

Now what we may regard as short-term memory—in other words memories which last at most for some seconds and which allow us to look at a scene, now closely, now distantly, now from one angle and now from another, and yet establish full continuity of experience—can probably be accounted for by continuously circulating chains of impulses round complex closed circuits in the brain. There seem, however, to be very great difficulties in regarding these as the basis of long-term memories, and it is probable that certain of these circulating chains of impulses give rise to permanent modifications of physical structure which enable them to be reactivated later.[1]

Can we, then, find any correlation between, on the one hand, the states of this most complex of neuronal networks and on the other, the states of consciousness and of unconsciousness? Apparently we can. 'There is much experimental evidence indicating that unconsciousness occurs when the patterned activity of the neuronal net is depressed'.[2] Before any neuronal pathway is opened a certain critical potential must be reached. When the level of activity in the cortex is low (or alternatively, as in the case of convulsions for instance, extremely high), few of the neurones are poised on the verge of this critical potential. When, however, the brain is functioning in the way which is

---

[1] I am uncertain whether all memories are to be so accounted for, if the speculations in Chapter XXVII are accepted.

[2] *The Neurophysiological Basis of Mind*, p. 282. Oxford, 1953.

normal for a person who is fully conscious, considerable numbers of neurones must be critically poised. In this state significant patterns can rapidly develop.

Now on the interpretation which I have put forward, as yet tentatively, there is a non-physical medium, whose behaviour provides the physical world. (It is the behaviour which is significant because the sense-mechanisms respond to the behaviour of the medium and not to the medium itself.) In the case of a living organism the form taken by the medium is that of a self-sustaining, self-regulating open system. This extremely complicated system brings together in the brain information from the surroundings, and the system in this critical centre is so poised that when conscious it responds to these constantly differentiated messages; when unconscious—for instance, asleep—it does not respond to them. Consciousness itself I am thus regarding as a property of the medium when the latter is so organized, and the objects of consciousness are the patterns of behaviour of the medium itself in a certain key part of the organization (the cortex) which itself is responsive to behaviour elsewhere.

Plainly, my arguments still need to be put on a wider and firmer basis, for so far I have treated the medium only as a solvent of certain contemporary problems. Before I go on to discuss the more positive evidence for its existence, I may provide a brief interpretation of the nature of psychic phenomena. Three main elements of my argument combine here; my interpretations of time and of space and of the body-mind relationship.

VIII

A Preliminary note on Psychic Phenomena

PSYCHIC phenomena lie almost completely outside our system of beliefs and explanations of them remain inadequate and unrelated to current thought. Accordingly they have usually been disregarded or explained away. The evidence is, nevertheless, too powerful for the existence of certain of these phenomena to be seriously doubted. This, however, is no place to justify this assertion: a good deal of evidence is brought together and discussed in two easily accessible books by the late G. N. M. Tyrrell.[1]

I may give here, however, a very brief indication of the way in which the arguments which I have been putting forward provide the basis for a comprehensive explanation of the phenomena and at the end of the book I shall add to this some further explanation and speculation.

The first and major obstacle to understanding these phenomena lies in the tendency to regard mind as an epiphenomenon of matter. The interpretation which I have put forward has been very different from this, and in particular, I have given grounds for postulating the existence of a substance or medium whose behaviour, abstracted from the medium itself, forms the

[1] *The Personality of Man*—Pelican Books, 1946. *Apparitions*—revised edn. Duckworth, 1953.

physical world. Accordingly, since I have given grounds for holding that space is a concept deriving from our experience of the spatial relationships between physical objects, and the physical objects can themselves be regarded as patterns of behaviour of the medium, we have not the slightest reason for assuming that space applies to, or limits, the medium itself. To put this point more simply in its immediate context, we can say that mental events do not themselves exist in space: space has no application to them.

Accordingly, in so far as the various psychical phenomena are mental events, it seems that the logical (though not perhaps the conceptual) difficulties in the way of understanding why they should appear unaffected by distance disappear.

There are, however, also major difficulties about time, and in particular, there are those of pre-cognition. These difficulties are for most people greater than those of space. I have, however, indicated that time is a concept derived from the vast system of change which constitutes the physical universe. The mind derives the concept of time from the changes occurring in the physical world. The medium, however, is itself timeless: our experience of change, and so of time, derives from its forms; time simply does not apply to the medium itself. As I indicated earlier, there appear to be good grounds for saying this, though such an idea must stretch our understanding to the uttermost.

Now if one mind is distinguished from another mind neither by time nor by space, it is presumably distinguished by its own continuity of experience, by its memories, and by its own preoccupations with what is happening in its own system. Accordingly, it would seem that the major reasons preventing one mind from establishing contact with another by para-normal means, will be the difficulty of actually breaking through the preoccupations of that mind. It is presumably when these difficulties are overcome that there occurs telepathy—which was defined by F. W. H. Myers, who coined the word, as 'the communication of impressions of any kind from one mind to another, independently of the recognized channels of sense.'

This discussion, brief as it has been, throws yet further light on the nature and attributes of the medium. It underlies all matter and in suitable states of organization it has the properties of life and mind; neither time nor space apply to it nor limit it. These properties are, however, some of the attributes which have been ascribed to God.

This identification will be borne out when I consider the evidence deriving from the experiences of mystics. It is to this evidence and to evidence from the aesthetic experience, from primitive thought and from nature mysticism that I must now turn; for as I have already shown, no positive evidence for the existence or nature of the medium can come from a study of the physical world. The evidence of mystics has, however, had certain serious criticisms levelled against it, and these I must necessarily consider first.

IX

The Significance of Mysticism

MANY millions of people throughout the world believe implicitly in the teachings of their churches which are to them infallible, and in the teachings of a book which they believe to be divinely inspired. For many others, however, the assumptions necessary to this attitude are quite unacceptable, and refusing the help and guidance so offered, they must continue their way either denouncing as mere self-delusion any attempt to find a reality more ultimate than man himself, or else, not so sure that the answer is so simple, they must try to find their own answers. Some such seekers are easily satisfied, others not so easily, but nearly all find some *modus vivendi* with their doubts.

There is no need here to go over the reasons which prevent their accepting as infallible either church or book. Ultimately such acceptance usually rests on an act of faith in which the help which reason provides is slight. There is, however, a third source of guidance which cannot, in this context, be dismissed so shortly, and this is the testimony of mystics. The word 'mystic' has however been used in many different senses and we shall presently have to describe more precisely the experiences to which we are referring. It may suffice at this point simply to quote Aldous Huxley, 'The technique of mysticism, properly practised, may result in the direct intuition of, and union with, an ultimate spiritual reality that is perceived as simultaneously beyond the self and in some way within it.'

There have been mystics in many ages and many civilizations: Christianity, Buddhism, Mohammedanism, Taoism, Neo-Platonism—all have had their mystics. The discipline which a would-be mystic must undergo is usually so arduous that exceptional zeal is necessary. Thus mysticism undoubtedly lends itself to self-delusion arising from abnormal psychological states. Probably most of the experiences of most of those who have claimed to be mystics, particularly where they have violent physical manifestations, can be so accounted for. There remain mystics whose experiences cannot be so dismissed and who though they have the greatest difficulty in describing their experiences, have no doubt that they have been in touch with the ultimate nor do they doubt their vital importance and significance of their experiences.

Now one of the most formidable attacks on the testimony of mystics comes from the logical positivists; we may let Professor Ayer speak for himself:[1]

'We do not deny *a priori* that the mystic is able to discover truths by his own special methods. We wait to hear what are the propositions which embody his discoveries, in order to see whether they are verified or confuted by our empirical observations. But the mystic, so far from producing propositions which are empirically verified, is unable to produce any intelligible

[1]*Language, Truth and Logic*, 2nd edn., pp. 118–19. Gollancz, 1950.

propositions at all. And therefore we say that his intuition has not revealed to him any facts. It is no use his saying that he has apprehended facts but is unable to express them. For we know that if he really had acquired any information, he would be able to express it. He would be able to indicate in some way or other how the genuineness of his discovery might be empirically determined. The fact that he cannot reveal what he "knows", or even himself devise an empirical test to validate his "knowledge". shows that his state of mystical intuition is not a genuinely cognitive state. So that in describing his vision the mystic does not give us any information about the external world; he merely gives us indirect information about the condition of his own mind.'

Now, if I interpret Professor Ayer correctly he demands that the mystic should satisfy the following conditions:

(a) he should be able to describe his experiences in intelligible form;

(b) his discoveries as so described should be capable of being verified by our empirical observations.

There is also, it would seem, implicit in this statement the belief that since the information which the mystic conveys to us is not about the external world, it must therefore be regarded as of no general significance.

Now for the description of an experience to be intelligible either we must have experienced it ourselves or it must be described, either as a whole or by aspects, in terms of something we already know. The experiences of mystics are, however, given to few people, so that few people can substantiate the testimony of a mystic by their own experience. Further, the testimony of mystics is of something which is apparently so dissimilar to our everyday experiences that it is not possible to find adequate parallels to describe it. The difficulty is comparable to that of describing colour to a blind man, and this is hardly greater than the problem of describing colour to anyone (except in terms of other colours). The experiences of mystics are not sense-experiences, however, nor, it would seem, are they really similar to them. They are apparently experiences which engulf the entire consciousness of the individual, completely transcending it: experiences which, pregnant with meaning, affect the entire consciousness of the mystic, and yet are completely undifferentiated. Obviously, then, if this is their nature, we cannot expect mystics to indicate their nature to us unless we have already had these experiences, or something comparable, ourselves; nor can they adequately describe them. This is not only because most people know nothing similar, but also because it would be impossible to describe (as distinct from indicate) something which is undifferentiated and apparently transcends the bounds of all knowledge, for all information must in some measure be defined. In these circumstances it is hardly surprising, since the experiences of the mystic are so unusual and so unlike any other experience, that they cannot be described intelligibly, for they are in their nature rare and abnormal.

That such experiences as these do not give us information about the external world is clear, but this they do not profess to do. As Professor Ayer says, the experience of the mystic cannot be denied, but only its significance—and its significance can be denied *a priori* only in a wider context. Thus one may postulate that only knowledge which derives ultimately from the senses is knowledge which can be accepted in building up a picture of the universe; such a postulate, however, unless arbitrary, must rest ultimately only on one's understanding of the universe as a whole—in short, on a particular metaphysic. In so far as there is any doubt or uncertainty about such a metaphysic the less can the arbitrary dismissal of such experiences be justified.

It is hard to conceive of what Professor Ayer has in mind when he speaks of testing experiences of mystics empirically. After all, we can only test empirically someone else's experience of blueness by his behaviour or by his description of it in terms of parallels we ourselves have experienced, and if we have not had the sensation of blueness ourselves and do not accept the testimony of others who have, it is not easy to see how we can test it; similarly with mysticism. However, I hope to show later that an empirical test—that of personal experience—though of great difficulty, is in theory quite possible to any man.

Naturally, however, by moving the arbitrary bar to the consideration of the evidence of mystics, one does not thereby establish that any significance does attach to it. Further, its significance cannot, in its nature, be established by reference to the direct experiences of all or even many men. The weighing of such evidence is much more akin to the weighing of the evidence of history. We have many testimonies from many individuals from many different parts of the world in many different ages. The weight of such evidence can never be conclusive, but at best can only be cumulative. It is only when the cumulative weight of such evidence is combined with other evidence, and the whole is woven into an interpretation or hypothesis which accounts, not only for the evidence of everyday experience and of science, but also for these more special experiences, that we can expect them to be treated as of any great significance. This is also in large measure the answer which must be made to those who would dismiss the experiences of mystics more especially as psychological aberrations. These criticisms, however, deserve a more detailed consideration.

X

Psychology and Mysticism

THE study of psychology has one obvious but, in the context of this book, significant limitation. No psychologist can experience directly what his patient experiences. Our experiences are ours alone: no one can think my thoughts, dream my dreams, feel my feelings or in general experience my experiences, whatever my mental state. It is true that if these experiences are of such a nature that they would derive from physical objects and so be available to other people—if, for example, a patient says he has been visited by some well-known person who has been nowhere near—then, plainly, his experience would be of a type which is public, and it can be assessed accordingly. But if I say I am hearing strange voices, though I can be assured that it is my imagination, no one can say I am not hearing them. Likewise if on recovery from a particular state of madness an individual relates the wonderful experiences he has had, no one can deny that he had them.

Experiences of this type occur to sufferers from certain forms of madness, and by way of example we may consider some of the characteristics of the behaviour and experience of people suffering from manic-depressive psychoses.[1] The characteristics of a manic

[1]A graphic and important account of this illness is given in *Wisdom, Madness and Folly* by John Custance, Gollancz, 1950.

phase of the illness are described by G. Zilboorg thus:[1]

'A patient in a manic attack presents a very typical picture. He is unusually cheerful, extremely free in speech and action; he lives as if under a gigantic pressure of physical and mental activity. He hardly has time to dwell for a minute on any one thing. No sooner does he capture (show interest in) one thing, than he jumps to another; he is distractable, verbose, flighty, volatile. Nothing disturbs his glorious sense of well-being. Nothing seems to tire him, embarrass him. He is unusually frank and open, strikingly un-conventional in speech and manner—no matter how formal and straight-laced his upbringing, and no matter how inhibited he might have been before the manic attack. He seems to live in a constant, orgiastic state of celebrating the glory of all his impulses. The whole mass of his instinctual impulses (id) seems to have broken through the barrage of conventional conscience (super-ego) and to have dismantled the apparatus which tests and deals with the realities of life (ego). One might say that the individual in a manic attack presents almost nothing else but a bundle of happily sparkling primitive instinctual drives.'

As Freud himself has said: 'We see that the manic patient has thrown off the yoke of his super-ego, which now no longer takes up a critical attitude towards the ego, but has become merged in it.' The union of ego and super-ego obviously brings a sense of immense

[1]'Manic-depressive psychoses', an essay in *Psycho-Analysis Today*, edited by Sandor Lorand, published in Great Britain by Allen & Unwin Ltd., 1948, p. 271.

power and harmony, but while the attack lasts this is at the expense of all normal contact with the world around him. He has a greatly heightened sense of reality with intensified sense-impressions and a great sense of well-being. The barriers of individuality appear to be breached; there is no sense of repulsion; sexual and moral tension is relaxed; the patient has delusions of grandeur and power. Above all, he may on occasions have a sense of ineffable revelation, a sense of mystery unveiled and of wisdom becoming certain beyond all possibility of doubt. Time seems no longer real and evil seems not real but mere appearance. In particular there is a profound sense of the unity of all things, reconciling all conflicts, and all opposition, in an ineffable unity. As we shall see, there is thus a marked similarity between this latter aspect of the experiences of certain patients in the full manic phase of their illness and the highest levels of religious insight which are attained in the mystical experience.

Before they have attained such experience, moreover, a number of mystics have experienced the state known as 'the dark night of the soul' which bears a great similarity to certain aspects of the experiences of a patient in the depressive phase of his illness.[1]

[1]In this phase the condition of the patient is completely different from his condition in the manic phase. He suffers from extreme depression and sense of sin; he accuses himself of numerous unpardonable crimes; his conscience may take hallucinatory form and he may hear the reproaches and abuse being hurled upon him. The world seems utterly evil; everything is black and menacing.

William James has well described the feelings of a patient in this state: 'Desperation absolute and complete, the whole universe

Experiences of rather similar nature to those which occur in the manic phase occur sometimes in other states of madness and in other abnormal circumstances. One of these experiences is 'anaesthetic revelation' which sometimes affects persons inhaling ether or nitrous oxide. The experience bears some relation to the experiences of alcohol and drug addicts but is very much more intense. The person who inhales feels he has revealed to him depth upon depth of truth, and its keynote is invariably unity and reconciliation. On returning to a consciousness, the experience fades unaccountably, though a sense of profound meaning remains.

These experiences have no counterpart in the external world, though their effects on the behaviour of the patient can, of course, be observed; there are no means whereby we can conclusively confirm or deny these experiences, but there is ample testimony that they occur. What can most reasonably be questioned is whether any significance should be attached to them. Though the experiences are certainly abnormal, that

---

coagulating about the sufferer into a material of overwhelming horror, surrounding him without opening or end. Not the conception of intellectual perception of evil, but the grisly, blood-freezing, heart paralysing sensation of it close upon me, and no other conception or sensation able to live for a moment in its presence.'

In this state it would seem that the distinction between the ego and the super-ego becomes very marked, and the latter increases its power greatly, particularly in its authoritarian and aggressive aspects. The super-ego, in short, seems to come between the id and the ego to a quite abnormal extent, and punishes ruthlessly and sadistically every attempt to gratify the demands of the id.

in itself is no criterion of significance. Whether something has significance depends upon the context in which it is judged. These experiences can be judged as of no significance only when one has first adopted a conception of reality in which they find no significant place. There have been many conceptions as to the nature of reality, but although faults and contradictions have been found in most of them, and some have proved more successful than others in placing within a single scheme all the multiple experiences of our lives, yet no one scheme seems for long to have established itself as a complete and satisfying metaphysic acceptable to all reasonable people.

Accordingly when I have reason in later pages to describe mystical experiences which are given to but few people, it is important that it should be realized, before they are dismissed as hallucinations or as madness, that, in so far as this means that they are abnormal, this is undoubted, but that abnormality is no criterion as to their significance; this can be judged only in the context of some particular conception of the universe, to which few people nowadays would claim to have found the key. That the mystical experiences have something in common with certain forms of madness, I have stressed; but it does not follow that they can accordingly be dismissed as unimportant. There are vitally significant differences between the great mystics and manic-depressives.

XI

The Evidence of Mystics

THE testimonies of mystics agree to a remarkable extent, irrespective of country, religion or period. They differ mainly on the value and significance of the sensed world of time and space. The real mystic is a rare individual—perhaps as rare as the great poet, artist or musician. Plotinus says that the power of spiritual perception is one that few use but all possess; but the qualities of mind that are needed by the great mystics ensure that few can reach their state. As we shall have cause to remark later, strong intellectual and moral qualities are called for, not only for the mystic state to be attained, but also for the experience to be transmuted into permanent and communicable form. Even then, in so far as the experience of the religious mystic is enshrined in precepts or in dogma, the essential nature of the experience tends to become diluted over time and space, and unless constantly renewed, it leaves only almost valueless shells and husks to be grasped by the intellect without any real appreciation of their true meaning and significance.

Though all the great religions of the world have had their mystics, nowhere have the mystical experiences been more systematically and assiduously sought than in India. The records of these experiences and of the wisdom which was built up in the light of them, go back long before Christ. Although the intensity of the pursuit and study of these experiences would appear to have been greater, and to have become more deeply embedded in the life of the people in India than in any other part of the world, they are by no means unusual elsewhere. There is, as we shall see, a very strong mystical element in Buddhism which, although it originated in India, spread to many other parts of the Eastern world. We shall also consider some of the mystical elements in Chinese religion. Sufi Mystical tradition was of very great significance in Islam. There is strong evidence of mysticism among the Hebrews and in ancient Greece, and these traditions merge through into the intense mystical activity of early Christianity. Thus the Neo-Platonist Plotinus, whom Dean Inge regarded as the greatest philosopher among the mystics, had a very great influence in the development of Christianity. Nor did this activity disappear in later times, for the mystical element in Christianity remained very strong; the 'Via Mystica' was the well established path leading to the mystical experience. Although probably comparatively few individuals actually attained the full mystical experience, it was a recognized aspect of Christianity, and was in no way alien or unusual. It is, indeed, one of the remarkable facets of our time that within the last two hundred years knowledge of the mystical experience which for so long formed an integral element of Christianity, and of almost all the other great religions, should have been so disregarded and even spurned that it almost vanished from current comprehension. Even to-day, with the awakening interest in the evidence of mystics, knowledge of their experiences has remained almost completely unrelated to the prevailing beliefs of the age.

A variety of techniques of self-discipline and development leading to the mystical experience have long been known. The 'Via Mystica' of Christianity finds its counterpart in the 'Tao'—the 'Way'—of the Chinese, the Tariquat of Moslems, and among others, the various techniques of the Yoga of India.

This is no place to do more than refer to a few of the very many paths which are prescribed or the stages on those paths which are described in all the world's major religions. Each starts from the premises of its own religion and its own way of life. Some describe many stages and some a few, but in practice there seems to be no clear division between the stages, for they merge into each other and, though the evidence of progress is plain, the significant landmarks vary both according to the individual and the path he treads. Thus at the stage of illumination which is clearly much more frequently attained than the state of true mystical union, the heightened consciousness naturally concentrates upon and expresses itself in terms of the religion of the individual. Likewise, in attempting to recollect and draw conclusions from the mystical experience itself, the terms used and the intellectual framework into which they fit vary similarly.

For Christians the three basic stages of the 'Via Mystica' are the purgative, the illuminative and the contemplative. The purgative stage consists in the elimination of worldly interests and the stilling of passions. In so far as the mind becomes freer and more serene, spiritual activity and enlightenment increases. This second stage is that of illumination. It is the stage in which the individual and the absolute are still quite distinct but consciousness is much intensified. The mind is apparently unified and experiences the material world as of greatly heightened significance. This is the stage which in its lower phases, many ordinary people reach fleetingly on a few occasions in their lives; it is more frequently attained in the aesthetic experience; and the inspired artist often reaches it still more frequently and for more sustained periods.

The final or contemplative stage requires an extraordinary development of the powers of concentration, and, with the actual mystical experience, in which, as we have seen, all sense of distinction between the individual and the absolute vanishes, the culmination of this stage and the whole 'Via Mystica' is reached.

The 'Via Mystica' has as its counterpart in Chinese thought, the 'Tao' or 'The Way'. Though far from its central tradition, on account of their neglect of social duties, the practices of the Quietists illustrate the mystical element in Chinese Thought.[1]

Their great emphasis was on cleansing the heart by stilling all outward activities, appetites, and emotions. 'Through this "stillness", this complete cessation of outside impressions, and through the withdrawal of the senses to an entirely interior point of focus, arose the species of self-hypnosis which in China is called

[1]This is taken from *The Way and its Power* by Dr. Waley, pp. 44–6. Allen & Unwin, 1949.

Tso-wang, "sitting with blank mind", in India *Yoga*, "*dhyâna*" and other names; in Japan, *Zen*.' The techniques by which this state was reached were similar to those of India, and involved, above all, breath-manipulation.

'The process of Quietism, then, consisted in a travelling back through the successive layers of consciousness to the point when one arrived at Pure Consciousness, where one no longer saw "things perceived", but "that whereby we perceive". For never to have known "that whereby we know" is to cast away a treasure that is ours. Soon on the "way back" one comes to the point where language, created to meet the demands of ordinary, upper consciousness, no longer applies. The adept who has reached this point has learnt, as the Quietists expressed it in their own secret language, "to get into the bird-cage without setting the birds off singing".'

Plainly, to follow the mystic path is of enormous difficulty, requiring very great strength of mind and character. It is not the kind of thing to be undertaken by those who are weak either in mind or body. Yet, as we have seen, something very similar would seem to occur in certain forms of madness. If, however, we regard the mystical experience as an entirely natural phenomenon, this creates no real difficulty, for we have suggested that in both, an essential requirement is the loss of power by the super-ego. That in one case an experience, similar to the mystical experience, occurs to an individual who has lost contact with the every-day world and no longer has control of his thoughts and actions, whereas in another the individual may be well balanced and psychologically abnormal perhaps only in his ideal normality, is, in the light of what we have said, in no way an unreasonable idea.

The essential conditions which govern the occurrence of the mystical experience appear to be these. First, all the internal stresses and strains arising from the irrational demands of the super-ego must be stilled. In so far as the power of the super-ego is decreased the mind becomes more integrated, more calm, more rational and the field of awareness would seem to grow greater and more sensitive. Secondly the demands of the body must be quietened—something which is much easier to attain when youth has passed. Thirdly the mystic must extend and develop his powers of concentration to an extraordinary degree, until, while remaining acutely conscious, he excludes from his consciousness all sense-experiences, all thoughts, and all feelings. At that moment, in the state of pure, undifferentiated consciousness, when all the differentiated mental events have been banished from the mind, there apparently follows, not, as might be expected, nothingness, but the mystical experience.

It seems to come from the very centre of the mystic's being. There is no sense of subject and object but of complete and blissful union. The experience seems to carry with it a sense of transcendent awareness which in its nature lies beyond any possibility of error. As I noted earlier, the experience can in no way be compared to ordinary sense-experiences, for it is completely undifferentiated; it fills the whole of conscious-

ness with consciousness only of itself. However active
the preparations may have been, the mystic is in a
state of complete passivity and surrender and any
attempt to exert any critical activity would seem to
result in an abrupt return to normal consciousness.

The basic idea conveyed by the mystical experience
is thus in full accord with what is argued here: it is of
the unity of all things, of one all-embracing reality, of
which physical and spiritual form two aspects. Man is
formed of both aspects, on the one side being formed
by his relations with material things, and on the other
by his continuity with the spiritual medium which is
the ground of the whole universe and God.[1]

Plotinus, speaking from his own experience, sums
this up:

'We must not be surprised that that which excites
the keenest of longings is without form, even spiritual
form; since the soul itself, when inflamed with love for
it, puts off all the form which it had, even that which
belongs to the spiritual world. For it is not possible to
see it or be in harmony with it, while one is occupied
with anything else. The soul must remove from itself
good and evil and everything else, that it may receive
the One alone, as the One is alone. When the soul is
so blessed, and is come to it, or rather when it manifests
its presence, when the soul turns away from visible

---

[1]By way of amplification of these findings I have provided a
brief note on some aspects of mystical thought in India, for these
experiences form the basis of the highly developed philosophy
and religions of India. This will show how many of the arguments
I have been putting forward find a fundamental and integrated
place therein. (See Chapter XV post.)

things and makes itself as beautiful as possible and becomes like the One (the manner of preparation and adornment is known to those who practise it); and seeing the One suddenly appearing in itself, for there is nothing between, nor are they any longer two but one, for you cannot distinguish between them while the vision lasts; it is that union of which the union of earthly lovers, who blend their being with each other, is a copy. The soul is no longer conscious of the body, and cannot tell whether it is a man or a living being or anything real at all . . . When in this state the soul would exchange its present condition for nothing, no, not for the very heaven of heavens, for there is nothing better, nothing more blessed than this . . . All the things that once pleased it, power, wealth, beauty, science, it declares that it despises; it fears no evil, while it is with the One, or even while it sees him; though all else perish around it, it is content, if it can only be with him; so happy is it.'[1]

[1]Quoted in *Mysticism in Religion* by Dr. W. R. Inge, p. 119, Hutchinson, from Enneads Book 6.7.34.

XII

Aesthetics

LET us now turn from the experiences of mystics to aesthetics so that I may seek some further evidence in support of my thesis. This however is far from easy to do briefly as no part of philosophy is to-day in greater confusion. Nevertheless, it seems worth while to glance at the evidence, however cursorily, and to start with, I may consider the use of the word 'beauty'.

'Beauty', as the word is used in everyday language, is plainly applied in the most diverse circumstances. It is frequently used for instance to mean 'a fine example of the type', as when we say 'a beautiful car' or 'a beautiful shot'. Again, the word is freely, and properly, used about landscapes or cloud formations or about some women. And, of course, it is used about works of art. It is on these that aesthetics, the study of beauty, has, above all, concentrated.

And yet the word 'beauty' does not fit all great works of art very easily. The 'Grosse Fugue' of Beethoven, the 'Lamentation over a Dead Christ' by Giotto, and *King Lear* are accepted as works of the very highest artistic merit and significance: yet they are hardly 'beautiful'. Or if they are regarded as beautiful, this is hardly in the way in which the word is used in its everyday sense. Nor would most of those who maintain that these works are beautiful, wish to argue that there is no difference, or only a difference of degree, between their 'beauty' and the beauty which is ascribed in everyday usage to the landlady's treasures. For those who can appreciate works of art, the difference is far too fundamental to be obscured by language.

Of course, a work of art may be beautiful and of high aesthetic merit or significance, too. Many people would say that the 'adagio' of the Beethoven 'Choral' Symphony, or Giorgione's 'The Tempest' are beautiful in the ordinary sense of the word. But it seems clear that works can be of high aesthetic merit or significance without being beautiful in the admittedly very wide sense in which the term is ordinarily used.

I am not here concerned with the word 'beauty' as it is ordinarily used, but I am concerned with the 'beauty' (if the term be retained), or 'high aesthetic significance' (if a less ambiguous synonym be preferred) of works of art. Accordingly it is on this latter sense that I wish to concentrate in what follows.

It is however most necessary to be sure what I am trying to do in attempting to cut a way through philosophical doubts and to elucidate the nature of beauty (in the sense of 'high aesthetic significance'). Clearly, I am not seeking criteria by which we may identify great works of art: when we know such works well, we either recognize their significance or we don't. Nor, on the other hand, am I deeply concerned about when to use the term 'beauty'. Though not all people would apply it to the same works of art, we would not often have much doubt about whether our reaction to some particular work would lead us to apply the term to it. Rather, it would seem, I am seeking to understand the term. The doubts are about its implications: I am trying to place it in and relate it to a wider context of concepts.

The need for this is borne out when we think of all the different criteria of beauty which have been put forward. In the *Foundations of Aesthetics* by Ogden, Phillips and Wood there is a table showing no less than sixteen different *types* of definition of beauty—and presumably it would have been possible to find at any rate a nucleus of works of art which all, or almost all, of the proposers of the definitions would have agreed to regard as 'beautiful'; they would have seen the same objects and recognized their beauty but would have 'explained' their experience in so many different ways.

Now obviously some types of beautiful objects, such as pictures, exist as a permanent source of stimulation of our senses; others such as music, achieve this only when performed. But in whichever class a beautiful object falls, it must absorb our attention completely if we are to appreciate its beauty.

In the case of a picture we must be able to comprehend the design as a whole at the same time; in the case of a piece of music we must equally be able to grasp the form as a whole. We do this even more obviously in the case of a novel; though we are conscious at any one moment only of what we are at that time reading, what has gone before is alive in our memory and is colouring every further sentence which we read. But whether we have to extend our attention in space or in time, in either case, as we shall show more fully later, we extend it considerably more widely than is normal in our everyday life. Further, this grasping or comprehending of the form of a picture or a piece of music takes place at the level of perception, with curiosity, desire, or even any lively interest banished from the mind. If, for instance, in the middle of a performance we start to think about the music we lose the whole continuity of form—we interpose our thoughts between ourselves and the composer. Beautiful objects are thus perceived as complex unities, and all attempts at analysis are for the time being excluded. Plainly, however, the ability to grasp complex works as wholes without sacrificing their detail and complexity, is something which training can improve but not all people have the same aptitude for.

Let us now consider what happens when we read a piece of poetry. As I have indicated earlier, the form of each word (i.e., the actual physical pattern in the air or printed on the paper) relays itself to the cortex where it excites the wide range of associations (physical forms with their mental counterparts) which give the word its meaning. The form of the word 'symbolizes' or stands for all these associations. This complex of forms would appear in some way to remain active in our brains, though subconscious, for it colours and adds significance to each succeeding word. Further, the physical patterns or forms of *groups* of words have their own associations over and above those of the forms of the words themselves, and so, too, have the physical forms which are the verses and the whole

poem itself. At each level more and more associated
forms or networks are activated and these influence
the subconscious: they give meaning to and are
symbolized by the forms of which we are conscious—
the syllables, words, phrases, sentences, verses and the
work itself.

When we come to a piece of music we find the same
thing—every note, every passage, every movement has
its physical form relayed to the brain and awakens
associations which give it richness and meaning. There
is, however, no fixed vocabulary in music and so for
each person each form tends to have a fairly wide
range of associations, and since the physical forms of
music are different from the forms of words, their
associations are different, and cannot really be translated into words. Their meanings, in short, are
vaguer, and in that they are less specific, are richer,
too.

The work of art, then, is a complex hierarchy of
significant physical forms—forms which symbolize and
crystallize the insight of their composer. And since a
work of art is so constructed that each form is part of a
larger form until the form of the work itself is reached,
the work has formal unity usually of great richness and
complexity.

The first stage in its creation appears usually to be a
kind of pre-verbal feeling, or idea. Stephen Spender
describes it as a 'dim cloud of an idea which I feel
must be condensed into a shower of words'; Beethoven
speaks of himself as 'incited by moods, which are translated by the poet into words, by me into tones that

sound, and roar and storm about me until I have set them down in notes'.

This stage, while it may be enormously different in degree, is apparently not really different in kind from our own not infrequent experiences of getting an idea and then groping round in our minds until we can find words for it—and if the idea is fairly important to us, we are likely to be quite disturbed and to go on racking our minds for quite some time if we fail to find the words we want. It is the finding of words to express the idea which crystallizes it for us and relieves the tension.

But the words are physical forms which stand for or symbolize a whole range of associations: in cases where we are looking for a word we appear to have started with the associations and to have been seeking the form which symbolizes them. Plainly, however, it is not necessary that such a form should be a word or a sentence or an essay or poem—it might, for instance, if I had greater facility in using these media, be a drawing or a piece of music. Just as I grope around trying to find the right form of words, we might expect the artist similarly to try to find the right form of sound or line to express what he wants to say. This, of course, is just what happens—to get the form just right is for most artists a long and tedious matter involving many alterations, though naturally some artists are more fluent than others.

It would seem, then, that the artist is trying to mould his materials into a form which corresponds to the form in his own brain (and so in his mind, since they are isomorphic). This form in his brain stands for or symbolizes a number of other forms which are associated with it and which give it its significance and meaning.

When the artist has completed the work to his satisfaction, the reverse process should then operate if the observer is to experience it to the full. The observation of the forms of the work should stimulate the corresponding associated networks in the brain and give rise to the corresponding experience. Needless to say, we may often expect the associations to be less complete and in so far, the full significance of the work will be lost; and to some people and in some ages this loss will be greater than in others. Further, since we use words to express ideas both trivial and great, and we use other forms similarly—as a comparison of Beethoven and dance-music shows—we would expect the greatness and significance of a work of art to depend on the greatness of the conception of its creator, and on his skill in embodying it in the work itself.

If, then, we wish to understand what it is that has caused beauty in general and great works of art in particular, to be valued so highly, we must consider further what is involved when we speak of the greatness and significance of the conception of the artist.

The idea that artists are inspired goes back into time immemorial, and it is usually possible to distinguish *le vers donné* from *le vers calculé*. I spoke earlier of the pre-verbal idea or feeling which the artist embodies in symbolic form in a work of art, and quoted the words of Beethoven indicating its typically dominating and all-absorbing power. It has its own character and feeling and usually gives rise in the artist to great mental activity. It is usually accompanied by exhilaration and excitement and gives a sense of great power. It is, in a very real sense, a state where the artist is quite unaware of time. 'Nor', as Professor Bowra says in his lecture on 'Inspiration and Poetry,'[1] 'is this condition negative, a mere state of omissions and absences. It is strikingly positive. In it the poet feels that his whole being is enlarged and that he is able to enjoy in an unprecedented completeness what in his ordinary life he enjoys only in fragments with afterthoughts and misgivings and distractions.'

We need not here recite the instances by which Professor Bowra supports the passage we have just quoted. He goes on to show that 'Inspiration, according to many poets, creates a state in which they see as a whole what normally they see only in fragments as part of a temporal process, and are able to grasp from outside in the full pattern of its movement what normally they know only from the inside in separated and limited stages of development'.

He compares the condition of the poet with that of the mystic, for the condition of inspiration is often one of extraordinary illumination for which the poets use the imagery of light. 'Just as the mystic may have moments when he is flooded with something which he can only call light because it makes him feel that he understands much in an order of things which is almost past understanding, so the poet, in his ecstatic inspiration, feels something similar.'

[1]'The Rede Lecture', 1951. C.U.P.

It is this insight into the nature of things which the poet, in his most inspired moments, symbolizes in his poetry, as do all the greatest artists in their own media. Yet though the greatest artists have this power and depth of insight, where the insight is less deep, beauty may appear in much more modest garb.

The very idea of insight may, of course, appear mysterious, but it is what we might expect from the nature of the thesis I have been putting forward. This is most clearly seen when we consider what happens when our attention is absorbed by a work of art.

Whereas in everyday life, when our attention is concentrated, it dwells upon some restricted part of the sensory field, when we concentrate upon a work of art, we are fully responsive to the whole of a field which is highly evocative (because it is symbolic); and, what is even more important, whereas in everyday life we tend to treat each stimulus or group of stimuli as a cue to further stimulation or response, a work of art is treated as an end in itself. That is the fundamental difference between the conditions of everyday experience and the aesthetic experience. In these circumstances we concentrate upon the sensory field not in order to discern and weigh its implications, but in order fully to experience and lose ourselves in it. In a sense, however, the field of consciousness is self-conscious, or, to use the concept of the medium as I have been using the term, the medium is self-conscious. It is both subject and object, and this is what makes it so difficult to describe. In so far as attention is concentrated less upon the implications of the changing forms of the medium than on the forms themselves, while at the same time being widely extended by the rich symbolism and high degree of integration of a great work of art, there follows the considerable increase in understanding and insight which we would expect from concentration upon these manifestations of the medium itself.

Of course, for a person whose conception of human beings is limited to one of transient coagulations of animated matter, the kind of experiences of which I have been speaking are naturally almost inexplicable, or at best derive from the unexplained insight of the artist into the depths of human nature. Yet interesting as it may be to obtain insight into the minds of others, this answer seems not really adequate. If, on the other hand, insight into the minds of men means also insight into the nature of the ground of the universe and the source of all significance, then indeed there is room for all ranges of insight from the most trivial to the most profound.

This theory of art not only provides a reasonable account of the nature of beauty and adds further support for the idea of the medium, but also it provides an explanation of the basic link between art and religion and the artist and the mystic.

XIII

'Nature Mysticism' and Primitive Thought

I WILL now, very briefly, indicate some of the main characteristics of 'nature mysticism' and primitive thought as these provide yet further evidence for the existence and attributes of the medium. In the every-day hurly-burly of our lives, as I have stressed, we devote our entire attention to noticing and to thinking about the implications of the continuous differentiations which crowd in upon our senses rather than upon the experiences themselves. And yet, in the occasional moment of contemplation and tranquillity, many people, perhaps just once or twice in a lifetime, or as in the case of Borrow, Thoreau or Wordsworth, per-haps far more frequently, have an experience in which time stands still and a deeper significance in their sur-roundings dawns upon them. At such moments ap-parently their attention ceases to be absorbed by the everyday implications of the manifold differentiations around them; their attention is held by the differentia-tions themselves and they become aware, it would seem, of an underlying significance. These experiences are closely related to the aesthetic experience, although in view of the unorganized and non-symbolic nature of the stimulus, they are apparently much rarer. It may be, however, that for less sophisticated peoples, they have been sufficiently frequent to colour their outlook and pro-vide a much deeper significance to their superstitions.

There would seem to be some support for this, for primitive thought is not very far removed from the level of dreams and operates through similar forms. Primitive beliefs are characterized, not by lack of logic, but by inability to distinguish between agent and act and between cause and effect. Primitive man simply does not know an inanimate world. It appears to him overflowing with life and far from viewing it with intellectual detachment, he experiences it as life confronting life and as involving his every faculty in a reciprocal relationship; and since life has individuality, be it in man, beast or plant, in phenomena animate or inanimate, primitive man in his every encounter sees it as having individual qualities and will. The world is felt by him to be permeated with forces, influences and actions, which, though not perceptible to the senses, are felt to be tremendously powerful in the control of human destinies and natural processes. Man is seen always as part of society and society is always viewed as embedded in nature and dependent upon deeply significant cosmic forces. Man and nature do not stand in opposition, for natural phenomena are conceived in terms of human experience and that human experience is conceived in terms of cosmic events. It has been said that primitive man has only one mode of thoughts—the personal. Thus his experiences are not with 'it' but with 'thou' for he does not distinguish the realm of nature and the realm of man, which he has not abstracted from the whole.

Long before the human mind makes any attempt to explain or theorize about the things it perceives, but only dimly understands, it is aware of a distinction between the commonplace and the mysterious, between occurrences it can deal with and those beyond foresight or control. What is arresting or inexplicable in terms of the normal, is assigned to the sacred order and given a transcendental significance.

Since primitive man is so much more limited in coping with his physical environment and in understanding its workings, than we are to-day, he naturally relies far more extensively on supernatural agencies. As Dr. G. F. Moore says 'in a thousand ways the primitive is made aware that besides his fellow-men, friends or enemies, besides the animals which he pursues or which pursue him, in short, besides the things he is familiar with or more or less understands, there are around him other things that are outside his understanding as they are beyond his foresight or control'.[1]

For primitive man, in other words, the habit of concentrating upon the implications of his experiences has not advanced so far that the power to concentrate upon the experiences in themselves is lost, as has happened for most people to-day. For him, the whole universe belongs to one great system of inter-related inherent life beyond the sensuous. The distinction between subjective and objective knowledge is to him meaningless, as is our contrast between reality and appearance. In short, for him it would seem that the abstraction of the behaviour of the medium from the medium itself is less far advanced.

[1] G. F. Moore, *The Birth and Growth of Religion*, p. 9. Edinburgh, 1923.

XIV

Conclusions

I MAY now summarize very briefly the argument so far
as I have presented it in this first essay.

(1) Some of the limitations of our conceptual system
have become so manifest, that modifications to
it would seem to be urgently needed. Such modifications form the subject of this essay.

(2) The language of sense-data in no way alters the
facts of experience and for our purposes it can be
disregarded.

(3) Phenomenalism attempts to provide yet another
language, but since it too in no way alters the
facts of experience, it can, for our purposes, be
disregarded.

(4) Sensory qualities have been all but eliminated
from the physical sciences: it is the regularities
in the relationships or patterns of behaviour in
the world around us which form their subject
matter. The relationships have been shown to
form a hierarchy, each higher unit comprising
related groups of subordinate relationships.

(5) Our sense-mechanisms, too, are such that only
patterns of behaviour are relayed by them from
the world around us to the cortex of the brain.

(6) Nevertheless the physical world as so described
is less than the everyday physical world in one

significant respect, for in the everyday world we are not only concerned with behaviour itself but also assume the existence of something which behaves. Everyday language recognizes this: if the physical world is defined in terms of patterns of behaviour or relationships, the objects in themselves must be non-physical. It may be maintained that everyday language is in this respect misleading. It is, however, misleading in no empirical respect. The ground for considering it misleading must thus be doctrinal. Nevertheless, although there are grounds for considering a non-physical medium as a necessary condition for the existence of the physical world, I proceed to treat its existence as a hypothesis and to seek evidence to justify this.

(7) The concept of such a non-physical medium is shown to be one which *prima facie* would greatly help in making intelligible certain very important aspects of physics.

(8) There is a basic unity in all matter, whether living or non-living: the same units go to make up both. The difference between living and non-living matter is from this point of view largely in complexity of organization. Life and consciousness are not things; they are best regarded as properties—and as properties, not of the behaviour of a medium, but of the medium itself.

(9) Living organisms are complex open systems, self-regulating and drawing energy from their surroundings, as well as information. The focus of

this organization and information is the brain where events occur which are causally related to events in the surrounding world. The events in the brain are patterns of behaviour in and of a medium which is itself conscious. Viewed 'indirectly' from the outside—i.e., at the end of a chain of other physical events in our own or someone else's brain, these patterns in the brain are physical. Viewed 'directly', i.e., without any further physical events intervening, these patterns are mental. This interpretation is shown to fit in with a large amount of our physiological and psychological knowledge.

(10) Space is shown to be a concept derived from the distribution of objects; time is shown to be a concept derived from change. Since both are concepts derived from the behaviour of the medium, there are no grounds for assuming that they limit the medium itself.

(11) Since the techniques of physics are concerned with the behaviour of the medium, the medium itself is strictly irrelevant to physics as so defined. No support for it can therefore be drawn from physical experiments. It is a *sine qua non* of the everyday world, but this is not in itself convincing to sceptics. Accordingly we have to look in other fields outside science and everyday experience for corroborative evidence.

(12) This is found, in rather striking fashion, in the mystical experience of union with God, which has commonly been regarded as the profoundest

spiritual experience of man. On such experiences have been built up a vast corpus of philosophy and theology underlying great religions such as Hinduism, Buddhism and Taoism, and forming a vitally important part of Islam and Christianity.

(13) These experiences, though unusual and difficult to attain, are strictly 'natural' and open to any man, and there is no reason to believe that they do not occur quite consistently when certain very unusual conditions are satisfied. They have much in common with the more usual experiences of 'nature mystics' and with the aesthetic experience, and, to a lesser extent, with a basic aspect of primitive thought.

(14) Finally the way is opened, be it ever so little, for a rational interpretation of a number of other sets of phenomena, and in particular of psychic phenomena.

(15) The conclusion of all this may thus be stated as follows:

There would appear to be good grounds for postulating one basic 'medium' underlying the entire universe and all its manifestations. This 'medium' is neither physical nor mental but spiritual. Of this medium the physical world is the behaviour and from this behaviour we derive the laws of science. Consciousness may be regarded as a property of the medium in certain highly organized modes of behaviour. Thus, when the behaviour of the medium is so organized, that part of the medium which is involved is conscious of the behaviour of itself and so of other parts of the medium. The references to 'parts', of course, imply a spatial division; and space is a concept derived from our experience of the physical world, which is without meaning when applied to the spiritual world. Accordingly, we can simply say that from this aspect the medium is conscious of its own behaviour. But the attributes of the medium are those associated with God. We thus come in the end, to a strictly monistic conception of the universe, a conception of God conditioning himself.

The form of my argument in this first essay has been, then, to attempt to show that a non-physical medium underlying the physical world is assumed in everyday experience and language. Taking into account the uncongenial idiom of modern thought, I have assumed that this argument will, by itself, prove unconvincing, and accordingly I have treated it as a hypothesis. I have sought to show that the postulation of such a medium would allow a ready solution of the body-mind problem. Further, *prima facie*, it would permit certain phenomena of physics to become much more readily intelligible. The medium is, itself, however, strictly extra-scientific, for in its nature no evidence in its favour can be found in the physical sciences. I have accordingly sought corroborative evidence elsewhere

and have found support in the aesthetic experience, in primitive thought, in nature mysticism
and in evidence of mystics.

There is only one medium *ex hypothesi*. When
the physical world, and so the differentiated
world of change, is excluded from the consciousness, consciousness can only be conscious
of itself, for there can be nothing else it can be
conscious of, and this is what the mystics say.

When, however, the consciousness is, as it were,
conscious of itself, the mystics relate, one is also
conscious of the ground of the universe, and with
this *ex hypothesi* we must also agree. That this
medium should be spiritual in its nature need
not surprise us; it could not be physical, for the
physical is no more than a mode of behaviour of
something more fundamental. Thus the physical
world is but the form of the medium; the mental
world is the medium as conditioned by forms;
the spiritual world is the medium unconditioned.

Even this, however, does not express the position properly: strictly we should not speak of the
form of the medium but of the form and the
medium or substance of something which has
both. This something has the attributes of God,
and so we find ourselves saying what, from very
different premises, is said by Tillich, the
eminent Protestant theologian.[1]

'The being of God is being-itself. The being of
God cannot be understood as the existence of a

[1]*Systematic Theology*, Vol. I, pp. 261–4. Nisbet, 1953.

being alongside others or above others . . .
When applied to God, superlatives become
diminutives. They place him on the level of other
beings while elevating him above all of them.
. . . Many confusions in the doctrine of God and
many apologetic weaknesses could be avoided if
God were understood first of all as being-itself or
as the ground of being . . . On this basis a first
step can be taken toward the solution of the
problem which usually is discussed as the im-
manence and the transcendence of God. As the
power of being, God transcends every being and
also the totality of being—the world . . . On
the other hand, everything finite participates in
being-itself and in its infinity . . . if taken
symbolically there is no difference between
prima causa and *ultima substantia*. Both mean what
can be called in a more directly symbolic term
"the creative and abysmal ground of being". In
this term both naturalistic pantheism, based on
the category of substance, and rationalistic
theism, based on the category of causality, are
overcome.

'Since God is the ground of being, he is the
ground of the structure of being. He is not subject to this structure; the structure is grounded
in him. He *is* this structure, and it is impossible
to speak about him except in terms of this
structure. God must be approached cognitively
through the structural elements of being-itself.
These elements make him a living God, a God

who can be man's concrete concern. They enable us to use symbols which we are certain point to the ground of reality.'

In so far as this first essay has achieved its purpose, we may say, echoing T. S. Eliot—the end of all our exploring has been to arrive where we started and to know the place for the first time.

XV

*A Note on some of the Basic Concepts of Indian Thought
and their Relationship to the theme of this Essay*

THE basis of much of Indian religion and philosophy
is to be found in the Vedas—the ancient sacred books
of the Hindus. Each book contains a collection of
'Mantras' or hymns and a 'Brahmana' or body of precepts. In addition there are the 'Upanishads', mystical
treatises dealing with the Deity, creation and existence.
The date of these works is unknown, but the Veda
proper is older than Buddha who probably died about
480 B.C. Their earlier limit has been varyingly estimated
at between 1200 and 2500 B.C. They are among the
most ancient literary works of the world. Although
difficulties in interpreting the exact teaching of the
Upanishads gave rise to diverse schools of Vedanta in
later times, it seems clear that the prevailing view in
them is monistic and absolutistic. In other words
they teach that ultimate reality or 'Brahman' is one;
it is spiritual in its nature and everything else is explained as existing in and through it. 'Brahman' is thus
basically the same as the 'medium' which we have
been discussing.

The second most important trend of thought is on
the inner essence of man. The culmination of this
inquiry is represented as 'Atman' which is self, or pure
consciousness. Atman is sometimes described nega-

tively by denying that it is breath, senses, etc., which
are all not-self, and sometimes as the true subject
which knows but can never be known—'the unseen
seer, the unheard hearer, and the unthought thinker'.
In other words the Atman may be realized intuitively
but never made the object of thought. These two conceptions, Brahman, the eternal principle immanent in
and realized in the world as a whole, and Atman, the
inmost essence of one's own self, are, in the culmination of Upanishadic thought, identified as one. This is
tersely and clearly explained by Deussen thus: 'The
Brahman, the power which presents itself to us
materialized in all existing things, which creates, sus-
tains, preserves and receives back into itself again all
worlds, this eternal, infinite, divine power is identical with the *Atman*, with that which, after stripping
off everything external, we discover in ourselves as our
real most essential being, our individual self, the
soul.' In other words, the universe is the Brahman, but
the Brahman is the Atman; this was in essence the
conclusion and solution which I offered to the body-
mind problem. The full realization of this unity in
experience is the goal of life, and is conceived as the
overcoming of congenital ignorance by attaining full
enlightenment and one's true selfhood in Brahman. This
enlightened state is called release or 'moksa'. The
personal self of everyday life, the manifold ideas,
thoughts, imagination, and feeling, belong to the
relative world of the Many, but the true aim of man
is to turn away from this individual self and from the
sense world of the Many to the ultimate reality of the

Brahman, to be found within himself and yet more than himself.

This involves, however, much more than intellectual apprehension of the view that all is one; it means the actual realization of that unity in our own experience. The acquisition of such enlightenment involves, according to Upanishadic teaching, a long course of training—the extremely austere mental and physical training of the Yoga. The teaching was given only to true and tried pupils who had attained detachment from selfish interests. They had to have purity of heart and cultivate inner calmness and control of the organs and the senses. They had to preserve serenity of mind and they had to acquire such qualities as forbearance and concentration. Above all they had to be possessed of an intense yearning for liberation from the bondages of worldly life. Only a pupil with these qualities was suited to be initiated.

In the first place the truth as taught in the Upanishads had to be learned from a proper teacher; this was the stage of formal study. The second stage was that of reflection when the pupil had become intellectually convinced. It was only at the third stage, of meditation or 'dhyana', that direct experience of the ultimate was gained. It was at this stage, with the subtle power of the mind and the senses awakened by the practice of concentration and self-control, and giving increased keenness, depth and intensity, that the seeker became aware of deeper phases of existence, of the Brahman without knowledge of whom doubts cannot be solved. Thus the attainment of the goal of life involved a state of moral and intellectual perfection transcending the distinction commonly made between self and not-self, and between good and evil.

The Upanishads describe Brahman as having two aspects: the one devoid of any qualifying characteristics, and the other endowed with qualities. These may be equated loosely to the medium itself and to its behaviour. The unqualified Brahman or Nirguna Brahman cannot be characterized and is not directly describable by words. In the words of the Taittiriya Brahmana it is that 'from whence all speech, with the mind, turns away, unable to reach it'. The Upanishads abound in passages implying the total indescribability of the Nirguna Brahman and the inability of the mind to comprehend it. The Mahayana school of Buddhist philosophy has described Ultimate Reality as the Void (Sunyam)—in the sense of no-thing. A tangible object, such as a fruit, is only a combination of such attributes as colour, smell, taste, or touch. If these attributes are eliminated one by one, what remains is the Void of the Buddhist, and the Brahman of the Vedantists. Though unknown and unknowable, Brahman is yet the eternal 'Knower of knowing', and also the goal of all knowledge; Brahman is the consciousness that functions through the senses, but cannot be known by them. It is not in space or in time; it is independent of causation. As long as one is conscious of the duality of subject and object one does not know Brahman. The realization of this transcendent Absolute is an inexpressible experience in which the

distinction of subject, object and knowledge is annihi-
lated and they become one. Yet the Nirguna Brahman is not altogether detached, for it is the very
foundation of relative existence.

All this I have attempted to indicate about the
medium in the widely different contexts of the preceding chapters. It is the intangible unity that per-
vades all relative existence. It is, in other words, the
immortal essence of every man, and though it cannot
be an object of formal devotion, yet it gives reality to
the Gods, being their inner substance, and thus binds
together all worshippers in the common quest of
truth.

The Upanishads reveal a search on the part of seers
to discover the essential nature of the first principle of
the universe. They concluded that the essence of
things is not given in the objects as they present themselves to our senses in time and space, but that the
sensible world is only Maya, which term covers
'change' or 'behaviour' as I have used the terms.
Nirguna Brahman is the basis of that aspect of
Brahman which is endowed with qualities; this is the
Saguna Brahman which is conditioned by Maya.
Without compulsion from outside Brahman imposes
limits upon itself through its power of Maya, and thus
becomes manifest in God,[1] the soul[2] and the world.
Maya has no independent reality but inheres in
Brahman; so similarly, a fire's power of burning

[1] i.e., Mahesvara—the Great Lord: an epithet of Saguna
Brahman.
[2] i.e., Atman.

cannot be conceived as in essence different from fire. The universal self is identical with the individual self, and if Atman, the knowing subject in us, is the only reality, there can be no universe outside consciousness. Therefore the duality perceived in the universe, independent of Atman, is Maya which can be translated in this ultimate sense as illusion. From the collective or cosmic point of view, Maya is one; from the individual point of view, it is many. In both aspects it hides the true nature of Brahman, though this limitation is only apparent. The activities of Saguna Brahman include creation, preservation and destruction. Many sublime passages are found in the Upanishads, and other writings of the Hindu seers, describing the glories of Saguna Brahman. Thus in the words of the Mandukya Upanishad 'He is the Lord of all; he is the knower of all; he is the controller within; he is the source of all; and he is that from which all things originate, and in which they finally disappear'.

In later times differences arose in the interpretation of the Upanishads and a number of schools of thought grew up. Yet the goal of life, as interpreted in the Upanishads, remained in most schools a central feature.

The teachings of Buddha were greatly influenced by the Upanishads, and it is now generally believed that primitive Buddhism represents but a new expansion within Brahmanism, its criticisms being levelled mainly against its ritual rather than its doctrine. Two important differences from Upanishadic teaching were that while this was intended for the select few,

Buddhism was for the many. It has been described as a folk-gospel. Further, while the older doctrine relied greatly on instruction given by others, Buddhism laid particular stress on self-reliance and self-effort in knowing the ultimate truth. This ultimate truth is essentially the same as the union with Brahman of the Upanishadic teaching, and is Nirvana, the attainment of which is the state of extinguishment of selfhood in the ordinary sense of the term, but not the annihilation of self. The terms Gautama commonly used for the highest experiences of mystical insight were (1) Dhyana, the concentration of the mind away from the manifold of sense-experience, and (2) Samadhi, the absorption or concentrated effort of the inner mental life on to a purer sphere away from sense-experience and the mere externality of things. The two terms Dhyana and Samadhi were probably in use before the time of Gautama in the practice of Yoga, whereby contact with the manifold—the world of names and forms—was broken. The conviction had probably by then impressed itself on many thinking people that the soul of man carried within it the secret of the Divinity that ruled the Universe.

In trying to describe Nirvana the Buddhist is trying to express the ineffable experience where all contact with a differentiated sense-experience is lost. It is, however, described by positive as well as negative terms. There are countless hints in the 'Pitakas' (sacred canons) that Nirvana is not nullity. Gautama can find no term to express it because all terminology refers to the determinate world of everyday life.

Nirvana itself is known only in the highest mental states after strenuous psychological efforts. 'There are things', said the Buddha, 'profound, difficult to realize, hard to understand, tranquillizing, sweet, not to be grasped by logic.' As is said in the Dhammapada 'as soon as the Bhikkhu (mendicant monk) has considered the origin and destruction of the khandhas (individuality) he finds happiness and joy which belongs to those who know the immortal'. Elsewhere[1] it has been described as 'bliss unspeakable' and 'one of the most emotionally overwhelming, aesthetically ineffable experiences, with no sense either of self or of objects, which it is within the possibility of man to enjoy'.

[1] F. S. C. Northrop: *The Meeting of East and West*, p. 369. Macmillan, New York, 1946.

PART II

XVI

Introduction

In the first essay I have attempted to set forth, in broad outline, what is, in effect, the basis of a complete metaphysic. In this, the second essay, I shall have cause at certain points to make reference to this metaphysic: I shall attempt to draw support from it and I hope to contribute support to it, partly by showing further its general implications, and partly by showing how the contentions I attempt to establish in this part of the book find their place within it.

But though thus basically and integrally connected with the previous essay, this essay will be concerned with a widely different realm of philosophy: what may broadly be called 'moral philosophy and theology'. I shall first look very briefly at some of the findings and implications of psycho-analysis. I shall be concerned not with the more doubtful and esoteric portions of this study, but with some basic ideas, our application of which we owe largely to Freud, and which to-day are largely accepted by the man in the street, and even by psychologists who remain sceptical about psycho-analysis as a whole. I shall attempt to show, in particular, something of the nature of mental disturbances and conflicts and how they arise, and the characteristics of the ideal or 'normal' state of mind in which they are resolved. In order to do this, it will be necessary first briefly to indicate something of the nature and techniques of psycho-analysis.

Having established the main characteristics of the 'normal' (i.e., the ideal) mind and the nature of departures from it, and having related it to the first part of the book, I shall then briefly scrutinize some of the basic concepts of ethics. I shall hope to establish the source of standards of ethics, the grounds for preferring some standards to others and the ideal cast of mind from the point of view of ethics; and I shall seek to show that this ideal cast of mind from the point of view of ethics has the very characteristics of the ideal cast of mind from the point of view of psychology. I shall then show how some ways of life in some societies (and their counterparts in the prevailing casts of mind of the people concerned) approach more closely than others to this ethical and psychological norm. Finally, I shall attempt to indicate the place of evil and sin within this conceptual system, and to show that the cast of mind which is ideal from the point of view of psychology and ethics is also the cast of mind which is ideal from the point of view of religion—in particular, of Christianity. In other words I hope to show that in the ultimate the person who is at one with himself is at one with God, and, in the ideal society, at one with his fellow men.

XVII

The Nature of Psycho-Analysis

DESPITE all the great gaps in scientific information, the physical and biological sciences form a continuous body of knowledge. The transition from physics to chemistry, and through bio-chemistry to biology, is fairly complete, and within biology, both physiology and neurology have close links with academic psychology. Between academic psychology and psycho-analysis, however, there exists a distinct though narrowing gap.

Psycho-analysis grew up, not as an academic discipline, but as a practical therapeutic technique of the consulting room. It was primarily the product of the great genius of Sigmund Freud, whose interests lay, first and foremost, with his patients. By means of his techniques Freud built up a structure of fact and theory involving concepts and language very different from those of academic psychology. While carefully and painstakingly academic psychology has advanced our knowledge on many important though limited aspects of human personality, psycho-analysis, despite its limitations, has cast great beams of light along the vistas of the mind.

It has, of course, been strongly criticized on the grounds that it has none of the necessary precision to be considered as a science, and on the grounds that as

a therapeutic technique it is time-consuming and uncertain. But I am concerned with psycho-analysis
neither as an exact science nor as a therapeutic
technique but as a uniquely important aid to the
understanding of the motives and behaviour of men
in relation to themselves, to their fellows and to God.
Accordingly in this and the next chapter I shall
attempt briefly to indicate by way of necessary background, the essential characteristics of psycho-analysis
as a technique for exploring the human mind and of
the interpretation of its structure which has been
built up from it.

The whole basis of Freudian psychology is causal.
Freud saw that a causal explanation could always be
sought for mental events, no matter how trivial,
though often neither the cause nor its link with the
effect was open to introspection. The finding of such
causal explanations involved the doctrine of the unconscious mental life. He showed that, within the
unconscious is a residue of attitudes, desires and
affective relationships (cathexes) which were of importance in the early emotional life of the individual
and which remain active but unassimilated into the
personality of the adult. In the normal person, these
become obvious mainly in dreams, but in more neurotic people they obtrude in the waking state and dis-
turb the balance of behaviour, often in strange and up-
setting ways. Between the unconscious whose contents,
though active, are normally quite inaccessible, and the
pre-conscious whose contents can be recalled at will,
there is, however, no clear boundary. The mere pre-

sence of a friendly and tolerant person may make more unconscious material available to consciousness than would otherwise be the case.

The most important technique evolved by Freud for investigating the unconscious determinants of conscious mental events was that of free association. The process is essentially one wherein the patient relaxes completely and lets his mind wander freely in a state as far as possible removed from logical and directed thought. He is told to repeat just what comes into his mind, however irrelevant, trivial or unconventional it may be. This state is not easy to maintain and the state of consciousness of the patient varies from a level of near-hypnosis to that of logical thought.

At first conscious resistances deriving, for example, from everyday standards or distrust of the psychoanalyst, have to be overcome, but, after a time, particular and recurring trends of thought may be noted which are suddenly blocked by unconscious resistances. It is as though certain ideas had great attraction, drawing quite diverse lines of thought towards them. But these ideas themselves are not apparently acceptable to the conscious mind, for as his thoughts lead to them the patient may find his mind going blank and the train of associations ceasing; or he may find his attention deflected on to some less significant theme. These resistances may not be recognized by the patient but are very obvious to the psycho-analyst. They prevent the penetration to the consciousness of certain ideas, attitudes, desires and memories which, though unacknowledged, every individual has within him. These elements of his personality are evidently far from dormant and it is to explain their failure to enter consciousness that these strong forces of resistance or opposition must be postulated.

After a number of sessions in which he will probably do little but listen attentively, the analyst will begin to play a more active part, interpreting trains of thought and explaining them to the patient; all the time he attempts to bring the patient's ideas and fantasies into contact with reality. By this process of interpretation and explanation certain memories and ideas, which until then were being blocked, become conscious, and as a result, the unconscious automatic repression ceases to operate. These processes of de-repression and interpretation, though conducted on quite different levels of consciousness, cannot be separated, for, as de-repression gives access to further associative material, so this, in turn, allows the further break-down of automatic resistances. This process of 'working through' the resistances forms an integral part of psycho-analytic treatment.

Much of the material on which the patient is asked to provide free associations comes from his own dreams which were called by Freud the *via regia* to the unconscious. Freud's discovery of their significance has been a very important contribution to our knowledge of the structure of the mind. The dream, as he pointed out, derives from two conflicting tendencies: the desire for sleep and the tendency to satisfy a mental stimulus. The dream represents, according to him, the fulfilment of a wish. Such wishes are often primitive and may be strongly in conflict with our moral standards. When this is so, they provoke resistance and can reach the consciousness only in disguise. This, as we shall see, does much to account for the enigmatic character of many ordinary dreams.

The wish or wishes which inspire the dream are called its 'latent content', and the processes by which this latent content is transformed into its 'manifest content', is termed the 'dream work'. It employs mainly visual imagery, and to understand a dream requires a close knowledge of the personality of the dreamer.

It is in the nature of dream work that certain images should come to 'stand for' or symbolize persons or ideas or events which are of great significance to the dreamer; and psycho-analysis is largely concerned with elucidating these symbols. Plainly, however, both symbols and what they symbolize will vary greatly from person to person.

XVIII

Psycho-analytical Theory

VARIATIONS in the interpretations of the evidence derived from psycho-analytic techniques are of much wider significance than the variations in the techniques themselves. Freud's own ideas changed substantially. Both Adler and Jung broke away from him and established bodies of teaching of their own, which differ widely from his and from each other. A large number of psycho-analysts have remained faithful to Freud's teaching, but many others have deviated to a greater or lesser extent. It is, accordingly, quite impossible to present at the present time one interpretation of the nature and structure of the human mind which would command general assent. It is, for instance, only necessary to compare the structure of the psyche as envisaged by Jung with that of Freud, to realize just how wide the differences can be.

In this discussion I shall use concepts which are basically Freudian, however far they may diverge from his teaching in detail. There is, however, no necessary conflict between the viewpoints of Freud, Adler and Jung. It will be recalled that in Chapter V, I indicated that there are three complementary aspects of a living organism: the causal, the purposive, and the subjective. In no way do these conflict. The counterparts of these three aspects are to be found in psychology. The causal aspect is stressed by Freud who attempts to relate back mental events to the life and death instincts; the purposive aspect is stressed by Adler, who concentrates on the will to power; and actual manifestations of the unconscious in consciousness, such as the archetypes, are emphasized by Jung.

Freudian theory can be considered from three aspects. These have been termed the dynamic, the economic, and the topographical. From the dynamic aspect, psycho-analytic theory postulates two basic instincts—'eros' and 'thanatos', the 'life' and 'death' instincts which, on the one hand, motivate the organism towards self-preservation and the survival of the species, and on the other motivate it towards destruction and self-destruction. This division has given rise to considerable controversy and the existence of the 'death-instinct' has been doubted by many psychoanalysts.

Of the 'life instinct' there can, however, be little doubt, at any rate in principle. An organism follows a continuous course of development in time, from birth through maturity to death. Unless each individual is seen as part of a continuous life process, however, this life sequence cannot be adequately considered. Thus, from the point of view of biology the chief end subserved by each individual is to reproduce and to carry on the process. Necessarily, all living creatures have this reproductive function. Evolution works in such a way that successful reproduction, including, of course, survival to reproduce, is essential for continued representation among the flora and fauna of the Universe.

As might thus be expected, the prime importance of the reproductive and survival function in organisms is reflected in the psychology of human beings.

Since the process of psycho-analysis is one of bringing into consciousness ever deeper and more fundamental elements in the unconscious, we find, as we might expect, that the deeper the level explored, the wider is likely to be the influence of its contents in the consciousness and behaviour of the individual. Thus when a psycho-analyst works back from pre-occupations, which are, for example, plainly sexual in character, to more fundamental levels in his patient's psyche, these also receive the label 'sex'.

Even in its usual and limited sense, however, sex is of enormous significance, for it is a basic feature of our make-up, and since many instinctive patterns of behaviour can find much fuller expression in our civilization than those of sex, they thus give rise to fewer problems. But from whatever aspect of human life we start, it would seem that ultimately we get back to something equivalent to the 'eros' or 'life instinct' which motivates all living creatures. This forms one of the two fundamental dimensions of the human mind.

Now the second aspect from which Freudian theory can be considered is the 'economic'. From this aspect there are two principles: the pleasure principle and the reality principle. Both are concerned with satisfaction and the reduction of tension, but the former implies the seeking of pleasure or avoidance of discomfort by ignoring the disturbing aspects of reality, whereas the latter implies the seeking of satisfaction in reality itself. In Freud's view a characteristic of satisfactory mental development was the displacement of the pleasure principle by the reality principle—a process helped by psycho-analysis in that, as we have seen, it gives insight into the unconscious mental processes.

These two principles of mental life are not very adequately formulated by Freud, partly because they were not thoroughly revised in the light of later findings after their formulation in 1911, and partly because psycho-analysis started from the rather naïve assumptions of psychological hedonism. Flugel, adopting the terms of Bleuler, prefers to distinguish 'autistic' thinking and 'realistic' thinking.

Whatever terms are used, and wherever the distinction is made, however, it seems clear that both the pleasure and reality principles, or autistic and realistic thinking, are different ways of preserving the mental equilibrium of the individual; for 'autistic' thinking, for instance, usually involves a retreat from harsh and unsatisfying reality to the pleasanter and less disturbing realms of fantasy.

Now from a quite different aspect, we have already considered this dimension in living organisms generally. I showed that they are dynamic 'open' systems, continuously giving up energy to the outer world and receiving energy from it, whilst maintaining themselves, despite this continuous exchange, in a steady state in relation to their environment. In practice, of course, the organism is continuously being disturbed from its steady state, and is continuously tending to re-establish it. Past experience does, however, complicate this, particularly in the case of a human being; for the equilibrium of the organism may be regained, not merely by meeting disturbances arising from its environment, but also by retreat to memories and associations in which satisfaction may be found if the external reality proves too harsh.

But whichever way stability is sought, it seems clear that the tendency to maintain a steady state forms a second dimension of the psychology of a human being, a dimension different from but as basic and as fundamental as the life instinct or 'eros'.

Man, being subject to these two fundamental modes, develops as a result of his interactions with his environment a characteristic mental structure. This, the topographical aspect of the human psyche, was divided by Freud into three—the id, the ego, and the super-ego. Of these the id is formed of the basic instinctual and emotional drives of the human being which have never become conscious; the ego, on the other hand, is that part of the psyche which is in contact with reality and which moderates the drives of the id to comply with the demands of reality and rationality. In learning to control and protect itself from the blind id impulses, the organism develops psychic defence mechanisms to aid in repressing them. These form the super-ego. The super-ego is, however, blind and automatic in its operation, and it is the interactions of its different aspects with the rest of the human psyche which provides the major part of psycho-analytical theory. Furthermore, since the super-ego provides the strong impulses of obligation and duty, and since the reasons for my discussion of psycho-analysis are largely for the light it throws on morality, much of what follows will necessarily be concerned with the super-ego. Accordingly with this background on the nature and findings of psycho-analysis we can now consider in more detail its development and characteristics.

XIX

The Super-Ego

PSYCHO-ANALYSTS have distinguished four main elements in the super-ego. These are as follows:

(*a*) The ego-ideal: this is our conception of ourselves as we ought to be; towards this conception we direct a certain amount of self-love and in its attainment our self-respect is deeply involved.

(*b*) The precepts of our parents and others which have become part of our own outlook on life.

(*c*) An element of strong emotion which colours certain of these precepts and makes them of a strength and ferocity out of all proportion to the original precepts.

(*d*) A much more controversial element—namely a streak of sado-masochism which tends to combine with and reinforce (*c*) above. This element, whose existence is doubtful, I shall not consider further, but even if no account is taken of it, it is apparent that the term 'super-ego' is a wider and more formidable concept than that of the conscience.

Perhaps the most easily recognized of these elements is the ego-ideal. Clearly everyone relies to some extent —and usually to a very substantial extent—on the approval and support of his fellows. As Flugel says 'permanent and universal disapproval is a condition that is wellnigh unthinkable and unendurable, and no more appalling calamity can befall a human being than to feel himself utterly outcast and alone.' When we are young and completely dependent on our parents this must seem particularly true. In these circumstances we rapidly learn which reactions to particular situations are likely to evoke disapproval and which approval and we tend to orientate our activities accordingly. So there builds up in our minds a conception of ourself as we would like it to be and which would satisfy our standards—standards which, of course, we have adopted from our parents and fellows, and, to some extent, from those characters who have gripped our imagination from fiction or history.

These ideal conceptions of ourselves can, however, rarely be completely satisfied, if only because certain of their constituent elements will often be incompatible. Just as our childhood ideals of becoming cowboy and engine driver could hardly both be realized, so, at a more adult level, circumstances and the nature of the ideals themselves leave many of them unsatisfied.

Nevertheless, some of these ideals are of the greatest possible significance to the individual. They cannot easily be passed over and failure to live up to them gives rise to feelings of dissatisfaction, of guilt and of inferiority. The cure of a neurosis will, in a very large proportion of cases, involve the reduction by the individual of the standards which he sets himself and a truer appreciation of his own limitations.

When we have brought home to us how far short we have fallen from these standards, we experience acute humiliation. There are, however, a number of ways by which we preserve our self-esteem. For example, for failure in one field we may hope to compensate by success in another. A dropped catch may cause acute embarrassment to a keen cricketer whereas his inadequacies as a linguist may cause him no concern at all. Again, to keep in check one trait of which we would be ashamed, we exaggerate an opposite trait, as when an aggressive brusqueness covers a feeling of shyness and inferiority. We may, by restricting our aims, avoid humiliating failure; or by a process of altruistic surrender we may identify ourselves with the success of other people or causes and abandon our personal stake in the struggle. This process is most valuable in society and provides incentive to many devoted workers. It is, however, open to abuse in that it may, for example, provide a cloak for aggression.

The second main element in the super-ego is closely related to the ego-ideal—it is the standards adopted from the precepts, and moral attitudes of others. We can best understand this when we consider how these take shape in the mind of a young child.

The well-known work of Pavlov on conditioned reflexes is relevant here. He found that if a neutral stimulus, such as the sound of a metronome or a bell, is presented along with a natural stimulus to salivation, such as meat, and the combination is repeated a number of times, the sound alone will evoke a flow of saliva. In other words, a reflex response normally evoked by food is now elicited by a sound.

Something similar would seem to be an essential part in the process by which the child learns his way about the world around him. He learns to associate particular groups of stimuli which form the everyday objects and events of his environment, and he learns to co-ordinate his behaviour accordingly. He learns that the corners of tables and chairs are hard and that if he bumps into them he hurts himself. The associations so built up, though operating below the level of consciousness, tend to make his avoidance of such painful experiences automatic, and enable him to anticipate things before they happen. Likewise, the approval or disapproval of his parents are, as we have noted, also of the greatest importance to him and these he learns to anticipate similarly.

The occurrence of anything unexpected and disturbing, however, at once tends to make him frightened. Sometimes, for instance when a child falls, or bumps its head, it looks about it, and if no one takes any particular notice, it will perhaps whimper for a few moments, but then it will continue playing. This is often ascribed to its wily desire for attention. In fact, what has usually happened is that it has not hurt itself much but has had rather a shock, and it looks around for reassurance. If the world is going on normally, and though he has been seen, no one has shown concern, he is at once reassured. But if Mother, seeing her darling tumble, utters a shriek and hurls herself towards him to pick him up, since he is rather frightened and considerably uncertain what has happened to him, he is at once affected by his mother's fears and becomes terrified. It probably then takes some considerable time to stop his crying and reassure him. If this happens a number of times, then if he falls, even if his mother is not there, the fear which has been associated with the similar occasions previously, will at once be evoked. What is more significant is that for the fear to be evoked, it will not be necessary for him actually to fall. The fear will be evoked when he meets circumstances which he associates with falling. Similarly, if the child knows that, when he does something, he is punished, once again he will tend to be checked by the subconscious awareness of the consequences, and at the same time, associated emotions will also be aroused, particularly guilt.

Now these ideas on the way in which the child learns to respond to and anticipate particular situations are in no way unusual or unexpected. What, in practice, proves so surprising and disturbing is the strength of the emotions which are associated with certain of these responses.

By far the most important objects in his environment are his parents and he comes to realize that even when they are frustrating him, they are yet protecting him from the dangers of the outside world and of his own unbridled passions of whose limitations he has little knowledge.

The actions of a parent are, of course, of great importance in arousing these emotions. But the parent's own emotions associated with these actions, of which the child is very quickly aware,[1] are in a way even more important. When he is punished his immediate emotional reaction is usually rage with some fear, but the latter may at once become enormously increased if the parent's emotions are irrationally involved, particularly if some sadistic impulse is aroused. Similarly, if some action of his induces in his parent a strong emotional response of fear, this too will communicate itself to the child and its effect on him will be greatly exaggerated, for he feels his very relationship with the parent—a relationship on which he so closely depends—is endangered.

Thus, in the very process of learning, the child comes to anticipate the reactions of his environment, including in particular, the precepts of his parents in certain types of situation where their emotions are involved; and his recollections of these precepts will then, themselves, become charged with deep emotion and have a fierceness out of all proportion to the strength of the original conscious precept of the parents.

A further important factor in the orientation and strengthening of the super-ego of boys, is the 'Oedipus Complex'. The first object of love by infants of both sexes is the mother, and for both sexes the father is the first rival for her affection and attention. However, each parent has 'good' and 'bad' aspects, and the attachments of children of both sexes will tend to oscillate. Soon, however, at any rate for the boys, some

---

[1] I suspect that sometimes this awareness may be telepathic, as otherwise I find the explanation of how the child becomes aware of his parents' emotions, somewhat inadequate. (See Chapter XXVII.)

vague idea of sexual orientation appears to creep in. When one recalls the remarkable instinctive patterns of behaviour of certain animals, it seems not impossible that, even at this stage, the child has some innate idea of sex which he comes to identify in his parents. At any rate, in the case of many boys, the father tends to be associated with all the ferocious, revengeful and archaic 'bad' elements of the super-ego, while the mother becomes associated with the loving and pro- tecting 'good' elements. In part, the contact with reality will tend to modify these emotionally highly charged and fantastic conceptions. Nevertheless, neither becomes completely assimilated and they thus remain as internal, but alien elements within the self. The importance of these features in authoritarian per- sonalities we shall have to show in the next chapter.

Now the extremes of emotion which form part of the child's response to certain situations are naturally very distressing. In so far as he realizes from his experience that the extremes of emotion which he attaches to his recollection of the precepts of his parents are unjustified, these extremes will, of course, tend to be moderated. But, since they are so distressing, he will tend to avoid situations which give rise to them; or if he cannot avoid them, he will tend to seek some way of deflecting the emotion so evoked. Thus in avoiding the force of his own emotions, he will tend to avoid facing up to the normal sequel to the situa- tions which evoke them: accordingly he often does not experience their relatively innocuous normal sequel; as a result the association of the remembered sequels with all their highly reinforced emotions may fail to get broken down and will often endure with him throughout life, and distort his behaviour accordingly.

The question now arises as to how it is, if this account is correct, and this occurrence is at all frequent, that people so rarely manifest such emotion. The answers to this we have already indicated. Normally, people will tend to avoid situations where emotion is likely to become distressing, or alternatively, they will either meet with circumstances, or adopt a series of expedients, by which the emotion will be dissolved.

The most obvious of these circumstances is where punishment is received or meted out. When as children we feel guilty, this emotion, though it usually derives from the emotion of the parent, as we have seen, may be of much greater intensity. When we have been punished this emotion dies away, as did the emotion of the incensed parent who punished us. But the punishment need not, of course, be inflicted as such, for no matter how fortuitous they are, natural afflictions and hardships will tend to be regarded as retribution by someone with a bad conscience. Nor, on the other hand, need the feeling of guilt be justified; so irrational are these activities of the super-ego, that a person can feel guilt not only when in the eyes of the world he has done nothing to warrant it, but even when he has no conscious idea of what he has done to give rise to it.

Of the various ways in which the super-ego can be assuaged, one of the most valuable socially is by reparation. This satisfies the outraged feelings of the injured person, and removes the feeling of guilt of the culprit. Similarly, this guilt can be relieved by sharing the guilt by confessing and by bearing the reproaches which ensue.

Sometimes, of course, our guilt is lost to consciousness just as the guilty action and desires are forgotten. Sometimes, however, we can silence our guilty feelings by a process of rationalization, whereby we are able to find some secondary justification for our action.

In some ways akin to rationalization, but usually more sinister, is the process of projection by which we delude ourselves into casting the blame and responsibility for an action on to someone or something else, thus relieving ourselves of responsibility and passing elsewhere any need for punishment. This latter aspect may in turn get emphasized by our natural aggressiveness which can be allowed rein when cloaked in moral motives. This process of projection is, naturally, of very great social significance, particularly in so far as it allows guilt-feelings to be satisfied by an act of aggression. The punishment of criminals, for instance, often provides an outlet for our moralized aggression.

Now although such strong emotions may be dissolved in any or all of these various ways, since most people are aware of their shortcomings relative to the standards of their super-ego, many tend to have a vague feeling of uneasiness or guilt when they are exceptionally successful. They feel that things are too good to last—that when there has been an unusually good summer we must expect a harder winter. This fear of 'hubris' which the Greeks discerned as a fundamental human trait, has been of inestimable significance in human history, and a great influence against innovation and on the side of conservatism. It helps to account for the reluctance to get rid of pain and suffering which has prevented reforms on many occasions. For this trait Flugel has suggested the name of the 'Polycrates complex'.

The influence of this complex presents a remarkable story. For instance, the need of some people for punishment is satisfied by their hard personal circumstances, but if these change for the better, the sufferer may quickly succumb to neurosis. Some people unconsciously, but for the same reason, provoke hardship or disasters either from the outside world or in the form of various physical ailments, or they may exhibit a variety of obsessions. Not only do these various forms of punishment satisfy the Polycrates complex, but, provided the super-ego is satisfied in this way, some people can, without any feeling of guilt, do actions which they would otherwise regard as highly immoral. Thus if misery and hardship become too great the very strong restraining force of feelings of guilt about immoral actions may be much weakened.

All these various manifestations of the operation of the super-ego are present in greater or lesser degree in all of us, although we may not recognize them as such. Since they so distort our appreciation of reality, they plainly introduce a considerable element of irrationality into our lives. Further, they lead to conflict within the personality. There are three concepts (though the terms are not used uniformly) which are useful in considering the significance of these more or less discordant facets.

The first of these is 'adaptation' in the sense in which the biologist uses the term: namely the extent to which the behaviour of the organism ensures its own survival and that of its species. Thus the man who gets on in his society and contributes to its well-being is well adapted to it: the man who is at war with society is ill-adapted to it.

The second concept is 'adjustment'. I use this term to refer to the extent to which the individual is adjusted to the needs of his own personality and as a measure of his stability. In general, maladjustment and instability indicate a personality which tends to be unhappy in its nature; but plainly a person can be well adjusted to the needs of his own personality and ill-adapted to his society or vice versa, and in either event there can, of course, be much ground for unhappiness.

The third concept is the degree of integration of the personality. This is the extent to which the aims and activities of an individual are directed so as to combine together harmoniously or, alternatively, how far they conflict with each other. This dimension of the personality is initially independent of both adjustment and adaptation, but as we might expect, each of the three tends to react on the other two. Thus, the lack of adaptation of an individual will tend to give rise to internal conflicts; and thus to a breaking up of integration; and the lack of integration of an individual will tend to detract from his adjustment. The source of such internal conflicts will, of course, be the super-ego.

If the various ways which we have indicated of dealing with the emotional strains prove inadequate, this inadequacy can show up in extremely varied forms. They may be hysterical: in other words, they may by 'conversion' take the form of physical symptoms and may be even so severe as to take, for instance, the form of paralysis. They may, however, take the form of an anxiety psycho-neurosis as a result of an anxious defence reaction. Or again, they may take the form of obsessional neurosis, in which the emotion is transferred by the mechanism of substitution from the object which gives rise to the emotion, to some other object which is otherwise irrelevant and innocuous.

In most people, however, the various neurotic tendencies are not so obvious as to attract attention. Nevertheless there are very few indeed whose reactions and behaviour are not influenced by such tendencies to some considerable extent. Accordingly, in the next chapter I shall attempt to show this in the case of one particular and common type of personality in whom the super-ego is extremely active, and I shall do so by comparison with the characteristics of a person who is well adjusted and on satisfactory terms with himself.

XX

The 'Authoritarian' and 'Normal' Minds

I HAVE already considered, albeit cursorily, some of the devices which people use to quieten the demands of their super-egos. These are of the greatest importance to an understanding of their behaviour, and of morality generally. Obviously, some people are more affected than others, but almost no one is immune; for it must be stressed that these conflicts and the devices which mitigate or obviate them occur frequently in the lives of almost everyone, though perhaps they are more varied and less accentuated in English society than in many others. Normally, of course, these various devices which enable an individual to come to terms with himself and his environment are not recognized as such by him, nor are the motives underlying them. Plainly, however, to the extent that they occur they distort his appreciation of and his relationship with other people and with his surroundings. To that extent his behaviour is irrational; and he tends to be in conflict both with himself and with his environment.

All this has been brought out quite clearly by psycho-analysis and is well substantiated in many and diverse ways. Even someone as critical of psycho-analysis as Dr. Eysenck is prepared to accept, though with qualifications about their formulation, many of its findings. In the next few pages I shall attempt to sketch the main characteristics of what is known as the 'authoritarian' type of personality, as contrasted with the characteristics of the more 'normal' personality; and I shall follow closely Dr. Eysenck's own treatment of the subject[1] which is based on studies by research workers in America. Perhaps it is needless to say that it is unusual to find people who fit in with the account of either type of personality in all respects.

Dr. Eysenck first notes the contrast between *repression* and *awareness* as characteristics of personality:
. . . 'the extremely unprejudiced individual,' he says, 'tended to manifest a greater readiness to become aware of unacceptable tendencies and impulses in himself; the prejudiced individual, on the other hand, showed the opposite tendency of not facing these impulses openly, and thus failing to integrate them satisfactorily into his total personality . . . Among these tendencies, which are repressed by the prejudiced person, are mainly fear, weakness, passivity, sex impulses, and aggressive feelings against authoritative figures, especially the parents.'

The second group of qualities which Dr. Eysenck notes are the tendency to *externalize* as opposed to the tendency to *internalize*. 'The prejudiced person makes use of a mechanism which was first described by Freud, but has since been established on firm experimental grounds, namely that of projection. There is a

[1] *The Uses and Abuses of Psychology*—pp. 273, et seq. Penguin, 1953.

tendency in people to attribute personal qualities they themselves possess, but do not admit possessing, to other people . . . it is not the prejudiced person himself but others who are seen as hostile and threatening, or else his own weakness leads to exaggerated condemnation of everything that is weak.'

Dr. Eysenck goes on to point out other aspects of externalization: the tendency to avoid introspection and insight, thus rendering the content of consciousness rather narrow; the devotion of much energy to keeping instinctive tendencies out of consciousness; a tendency to strive for external success and status, so that there is less room for inter-personal relationships or taking pride in work as an end in itself; and the low degree of enjoyment of sensuality or of passive pleasures, such as affection or the arts.

'The non-prejudiced individual, on the other hand, being conscious of his own less acceptable tendencies, does not externalize them by projection, but integrates them into his personality . . . "His greater capacity for intensive interpersonal relationships goes hand in hand with greater self-sufficiency. He struggles for the establishment of inner harmony and self-actualization . . ." One of the results of greater internalization is a generally more creative and imaginative approach when compared with the more constricted conventional and stereotypical approach resulting from the tendency to externalize.

'This lack of an internal focus of the prejudiced person', Dr. Eysenck continues, 'leads to the next focal point of distinction, *conventionalism* versus *genuine-*

ness.' The prejudiced and conventionally inclined person generally seems to need external support in deciding what is right and wrong. 'This conformity to outside values in the extremely prejudiced person can be seen most clearly in his attitude towards his parents, which is one of stereotyped admiration, with little ability to express criticism or resentment. Many indications are usually found . . . that there is . . . considerable underlying hostility towards the parents, which is frequently repressed and which prevents the development of a truly affectionate relationship. At the opposite end, the greater genuineness of the non-prejudiced person is evident in his equalitarian conception of the parent-child relationship, which makes it possible for him to express criticism and resentment openly and at the same time to have a more positive and affectionate relation with the parents.'

The conception of sex rôles shows a similar division. For the prejudiced male, sex is, on the whole, in the service of status. In his wife he tends to require the conventional prerequisites of a good housewife. On the other hand the non-prejudiced man expects from his relationship with woman primarily companionship, friendship and sexuality. Similarly, the unprejudiced woman seeks primarily mutual interest and affection, while the prejudiced woman 'clings to a self-image of conventional femininity defined by subservience to and adulation of men, while at the same time showing evidence of an exploitive and hostile attitude toward them.'

The next group of characteristics distinguished by

Dr. Eysenck are 'power—versus love-orientation'. The conventional person tends to seek and admire power. A tendency to a ruthless opportunism combines with a comparative lack of ability for affectionate and individualized inter-personal relations. The search for love and affection are, however, much more important in the non-conventional person, who forms strong attachments not only for other people but for his work which tends to become a source of pleasure and satisfaction in its own right.

The last group of traits distinguished by Dr. Eysenck he terms *rigidity* versus *flexibility*. 'This is accounted for in terms of the necessity of maintaining rigid defences in order to keep unacceptable tendencies and impulses out of consciousness. If these defences are loosened, there is a danger of a breaking-through of the repressed tendencies which have not lost their dynamic strength, and whose abrupt or unsuccessful repression prevents rather than helps in their control and mastery. "An ego thus weakened is more in danger of becoming completely overwhelmed by the repressed forces. Greater rigidity of defences is necessary to cope with such increased threat. In this vicious circle, impulses are not prevented from breaking out in uncontrolled ways." A great deal of energy is spent on keeping these basically unmodified instinctual impulses repressed. This process, with its attendant projections and externalization, and its lack of internal strength and individualism, provides a rather labile and precarious balance, and in order to prevent it from leading to breakdown a firm, rigid, simple and stereotyped cognitive structure is required, with no place for ambiguity.'

These, then, are the main contrasting features of authoritarian and 'normal' minds. Let us now consider the wider influences of the authoritarian cast of mind, in which, as we have seen, the demands of the super-ego are particularly active. Of especial importance is the strong tendency to project these demands on to suitable authoritative figures, for obedience is easier than self-control, and admiration is easier than the attainment of the admired qualities oneself. Since the demands arose in the first instance mainly from the parents, they accordingly tend to be projected back on to the parents, but also on to other figures, such as teachers, or film stars. However, as the shortcomings of these become obvious the projections tend to be transferred to other more remote authoritative figures whose shortcomings are unknown or can be ignored, and ultimately on to God himself.

Thus people who are ridden by conscience tend to be obsessively loyal to authority and though they may behave in the way expected of good men, their deeper motives are those of fear of God and not of any love of him or of their fellow-men; they have a profound sense of duty to whoever may be in authority above them, but, of course, they demand an equally uncritical obedience to themselves by their subordinates. Such people are not perhaps very common in England, but, for instance, in Germany, this is probably the prevailing form of conscience.

Further, the characteristics of the people of any

society are usually reflected in the institutions of the society, and an authoritarian society is no exception. Thus authoritarianism will tend to prevail, for instance, in the family, in the school, in the political organization and in the religion of such a society.

In so far as religion may be authoritarian, there tends, naturally, to be great emphasis on sin and evil. The criterion of sin in such religions tends to be primarily in the disobedience to authority; yet, in so far as the qualities which we attribute to God are those which we ourselves have projected on to him, so far is sin not against God but against ourselves. In such circumstances, the more guilty we feel, the more powerful and authoritarian does God appear, which in turn emphasizes our feeling of utter depravity and powerlessness, and the need for complete self-abasement and contrition and disgust for oneself. This state can, of course, be relieved by confession or ritualistic atonement, but at the cost of accepting complete dependence on those who can confer absolution.

So strong are the prejudices and limitations of the strong authoritarian cast of mind that those who praise the perfect love of God may see no contradiction when they conceive of him as condemning the greater part of mankind to everlasting torment; and their impulse to worship may express a compulsive idealization of what is feared rather than a spontaneous gratitude to what is loved. But, as we have seen, the characteristics which are ascribed to God are projections made from men's own minds in order to provide a defence against an intolerable sense of internal persecution. In so far as our understanding of the natural world increases, and the confines of the supernatural contract, so far do God and the Devil appear less suitable to bear these projections from men's consciences and so men seek outside religion new objects to bear these ascriptions. It was such a void that Hitler came to fill for many Germans.

These then are some of the effects of a strong and authoritarian super-ego and the resulting efforts of men to contort their beliefs and personalities in order to comply with it. In so far as this brings the individual into conflict with his society, it gives rise to neuroses; when the limitations and alterations of personality are common to many members of society, they become institutionalized, and in particular, they are catered for by organized religion. It was this that led Freud to describe religion as a collective childhood neurosis of mankind and allows psychologists to regard neurosis as a private form of religion. Of course, not every religion nor every society, nor even every aspect of such a society or religion is authoritarian. There are also other aspects of these institutions which, though reflecting themselves in the consciences of their members, are more 'normal', for conscience plays a vital part in all social life; we all must of necessity accept limitations on our personalities. In an authoritarian religion and authoritarian society, however, these limitations are founded on fear and irrationality.

A number of psychologists have tended to associate the authoritarian form of conscience particularly with patriarchies and its unprejudiced form with matriarchal societies. The evidence for the existence of true matriarchies is however not great. The part played by women in different societies has of course varied very greatly, and even in strongly patriarchal societies women have their accepted rôles in which they are dominant. Since, however, the form of the conscience appears to be moulded mainly in childhood, the relations of the parents to the child and to each other are, as we have seen, of the greatest possible significance. In societies where the tendency is to regard the mother as the handmaiden to serve the father's will the influence will be very different from where the mother and the father in their own spheres are dominant, and the mother commands the respect of the father, particularly in the home and where the children are concerned. Of course, in any society, there are substantial variations from one family to another. In our own society, families completely dominated by the father and others completely dominated by the mother are by no means unusual.

It has been suggested that the societies where the dominance of the father is usual tend to be characterized by marked respect for law, by hierarchical organization, by an emphasis on rational thought, by an active and forceful approach to problems, and in particular, by a tendency to authoritarianism in the prevailing form of conscience. Where the mother is more highly respected, however, the drive of the authoritarian conscience is much less great, and the approach tends to be more one of passive acceptance of natural phenomena. The emphasis on hierarchy is here much less, too, and the acceptance of the equality of men appears to be more general; there is more emphasis on the happiness and dignity of all men and less on the importance of duty and obedience. The patriarchy is of necessity a restricted group; the greater influence of the mother brings a greater humaneness, less inner disharmony, greater equality and universality and a greater sense of peace.

How far such wide generalizations are valid is perhaps doubtful, but it seems clear that when the dominance of the father is less marked, the authoritarian super-ego tends to be less prevalent. The strength of the super-ego as a whole tends accordingly to be less great. In so far, however, as the strength of the super-ego as a whole is less, the more easy it is to bring it into relationship with reality.

As the super-ego becomes less important, so obstacles to understanding, such as prejudices, become less important, and so at the same time does sensitivity to rationally based guilt increase. Further, as the dominance of the super-ego declines and with it subside feelings of irrational fear and guilt, so there tends to vanish the need to evade the super-ego, whether by confession or rationalization, repression or projection. As a result, realism and reasonableness increase. The various neurotic aspects of personality, whether obsessional or of an anxiety nature, will thus tend to disappear and with them will fade irrational conflicts, hates and fears. In so far as self-deception is reduced, guilt will be felt if there is a basis for it, and will be eased by a strong impulse to bring about reparation. Rivalry will not be absent, yet it will not be ruthless; nor will hatred for that which is considered evil be absent, yet it will not be vindictive. These are some of the characteristics of the ideal completely integrated and fully mature man, an ideal to which ordinary mature men in some measure approximate. It is to the characteristics of such mature and 'normal' people that we shall find ourselves returning, in the following pages, as a result of our consideration of ethics, of politics and of religion.

XXI

Some Aspects of Ethics

ETHICAL judgements enter, implicitly or explicitly, into every phase of our existence. Yet there is no branch of philosophy in which there has been less agreement among philosophers, nor does it seem that any agreement is yet in sight. Nevertheless there have been many most revealing books published on the subject in recent years. In particular, a number of these have been concerned to elucidate the nature of ethical judgements and the logic of the language in which they are framed.[1] Their influence on my thought has been considerable, but any attempt to give any balanced discussion of their findings would be quite beyond the scope of these two essays.

My aim, too, in these chapters is a rather different one, for I am concerned, however briefly, rather to indicate the fundamental basis of ethical judgements

[1]Thus attempts to classify value-judgements as judgements about properties, or as purely subjective, or as imperatives have each been shown to be inadequate. But each has been partly right, for the attempt to classify them as properties draws attention to the fact that there must be something objective about ethical judgements if contradictions between one ethical judgement and another are to be resolved. The subjective approach shows their close ties with our feelings of approval and obligation, and the imperative approach shows their rhetorical force. Value-judgements in fact form a class of their own.

than to elucidate their nature. Of course, there have been attempts to do this, too, in recent years; there have, for instance, been theories which attempted to base ethics on natural science, and in particular on biology and psychology. But such theories appear to have been guilty, on occasions, of illogicality in that they appear to have assumed that ethical propositions can be deduced as a conclusion solely from non-ethical premises.

Since this is a snare which I must, myself, avoid, it is important that the point should be set out clearly. We cannot infer that we ought to do 'x' from, for example, the statements 'most people do "x"', or 'most people desire to do "x"', or 'most people are commanded to do "x"'; there must also be an acceptable ethical premise such as 'we ought to do what other people do' or ' . . . what other people desire to do' or ' . . . what other people are commanded to do'. Furthermore, this argument that we cannot draw an ethical conclusion from entirely non-ethical premises applies not only to psychology or biology; a system of moral precepts can not only have no complete dependence on science: it can have no complete dependence, for instance, on theology or history. Premises arrived at from such studies may, of course, lead to ethical conclusions, but only if one premise is itself ethical. Furthermore, such ethical premises must, of course, command the support of those concerned, and it has been at this point that many ethical theories have failed to carry conviction.

Now throughout the history of the philosophy of ethics philosophers have tended to lay particular emphasis, in their search for acceptable ethical premises, on one of two main aspects. On the one hand, there have been those philosophers who have stressed duty and obligation, and the rightness of obedience to moral laws; on the other hand there have been those who have emphasized interests, purposes and ideals. But all ethics of duty have recognized the existence of intrinsic goods and ends and all ethics of ends have recognized duties; neither aspect is completely satisfying by itself, nor are they in any sense contradictory; each is complementary to the other.

When we consider how, in practice we judge the morality of conduct, however, not only these two aspects, but a third must be distinguished. Not only are there rules according to which the conduct should take place and ends be pursued; there are also the motives behind the conduct to be considered. Let us then look at each of these aspects further.

When we can approve morally of the way in which, or the rules by which, an action was done, we say the action was right. We may, however, speak of a person being right to do something, or of the action itself being right, and these we do not always distinguish clearly. Further, the meaning of 'right' grades from the morally proper action to what is just correct without any moral connotations at all. If, however, we are speaking of a person being morally right in a certain course of action, this carries the implication that his motives, in so far as we may know them,[1] were good, and so was the end to which his action was directed. If we thought that his action was in itself right, but that his motives were bad, we would qualify our observation both by speaking, not of *his* being right, but of the *action* being right and then we would probably further qualify the observation by some phrase such as 'but it was fortuitous'.

Again, in order to say an action is right, we must have some knowledge of its end and this must be in some way worthy: otherwise we would not say the action was right. If a man gives money to an unworthy cause, knowing it to be unworthy, we would not consider he, or his action, was right; but if he did so believing it to be worthy, then we could say his action was right according to his understanding of the situation. Thus when we say that a man was right to do this, it implies that so far as we know his motives were good and so was the end to which his action was directed; but the main emphasis of the expression is that the way in which it was done was worthy of approval.

Now I have been dealing so far with the implications of speaking of the action of a person as right. I can deal more briefly with the implications of speaking of purposes or ends as good, and of the motives of the

[1] In all societies the same types of motives—jealousy, love, guilt, loyalty and the rest—are, of course, to be found. It is the incidence of these motives, and the actions which arouse and result from them which vary. But even within our own society, our discernment of motives is normally a rough and ready process: but one which psycho-analysis has sided enormously.

doer as good. Of course, when we use the word 'good' in everyday language we do not necessarily distinguish these two meanings of the word. But we would not normally say that an action was good (with the emphasis on purpose or end) unless we could at any rate assume that the motives of the doer were good and that the way in which it was done was right. The helping of a sick friend provides a good end or purpose for an action, but if the motives of the helper are to influence the way in which his friend makes his will, we would certainly withhold our praise. Likewise if the way in which the help is provided is by stealing, our approval will also be much qualified. Thus just as the judgement that an action is right carries the implication that the purpose and the motives of the doer are good, so when we speak of the end or purpose of an action being good we imply that the motives are good and the way it is done is right.

Likewise, when we say a man's action was good with our emphasis on the fact that he did it from good motives, if we view the way in which he did it as morally wrong, or the ends for which he worked as bad, we should again be forced greatly to qualify our approval.

Thus, although we may lay emphasis in any action on the good motives of the doer, or on the good end or purpose of the action, or on the rightness of the way in which it was done, in giving it our approval, we must at least have no reason to disapprove of the other aspects, for all three are implied in a moral action.

Ends, however, are not to be conceived if only as

static, as states, for many ends are in fact activities. Thus to help to organize the relief of hunger, which may be regarded as providing a good purpose or end, is not in itself a state but an activity. Also the end of helping to organize the relief of hunger may from one aspect, be regarded as a means—for instance to increase the happiness of the people whose hunger is assuaged. Ends and means are thus intricately related and are not strictly separable. An action which, when considered in isolation, may be considered to be good or right, may thus, when all other aspects are taken into account, be very far from satisfactory. Further, 'good' is not, of course, an end in itself, but a value which we accord to activities many of which have as their ends or purposes the solution of the practical problems of everyday life, and these problems vary from society to society.

The means according to which a given end can rightly be attained also vary from society to society, for in deciding on these means, regard will have to be had to the conventions, laws and moral principles that apply there. The importance of the way of life of the society in question is reinforced when we consider particular actions as examples. Thus whether we regard the killing of a man as murder, homicide, justifiable homicide, manslaughter, accidental death or an act of great gallantry on the field of battle, will depend on the context of the action; and often not only on the immediate context, but on the whole way of life in which it occurred. Likewise sexual intercourse may be considered right after the marriage ceremony has been performed and wrong before; yet conventions on these matters vary greatly, and whether a particular instance is to be considered as right or wrong can often be ascertained only in the context of the way of life as a whole.

It is true that among individuals who belong to our own way of life much of the context can be neglected, for it is presupposed in every judgement; but when we attempt to judge an action, or to understand the judgement of a person who belongs to another way of life the context at once becomes all important. As Professor Macbeath says in his recent valuable book on comparative ethics as revealed by recent anthropological studies of primitive societies, ' . . . what the view of the anthropologists really amounts to is that the simplest self-contained unit of conduct, which can justify or render intelligible a final moral judgement, is a way of life as a whole, or at least a very substantial part of such a way of life.'[1]

The evidence in favour of judging actions within the context of, and by the standards of, the way of life[2] of the society in question would thus seem too powerful to ignore. Certainly the ordinary code of standards of his way of life provides the ethical basis for the actions of almost every individual.

There are, however, particular actions, which,

[1] *Experiments in Living*, Macmillan, 1952.
[2] The way of life of ordinary people will often vary somewhat, and in particular cases significantly, from the rather idealized version which is currently accepted by the people as a whole. Such variations are usually evidence of lack of full adaptation on the part of the individuals concerned.

though judged as satisfactory within a certain way of life, cannot but be abhorred. Clearly, the way of life cannot itself provide the ultimate standard of ethical judgement. This would seem to imply that if, in order fully to understand and judge an action to which we object, we have to take into account the whole, or some substantial part of the way of life, and if having done so, we still object to it, then, since it would seem that it cannot be condemned out of context, we may find ourselves bound to condemn the context too. I am suggesting, in other words, that though we must judge actions by the standards of morality of the way of life in which they occur, the way of life of some societies will be better than that of others. What I am accordingly faced with if I am to establish a firmer basis for morality is the problem of finding criteria by which we may judge one way of life to be better or worse than another, from the point of view of ethics. In order that I may do this, however, I must consider more closely the relationship of an individual to the way of life of his society.

XXII

Ethics and Society

A SOCIETY is no more than the individuals who make it up and who act according to a very complex pattern of behaviour. In any society there must, of course, be rules of behaviour which may be variously classified as good manners, duties, laws or divine requirements. If people live together they must recognize certain 'musts' and 'must-nots'. This working together and live-and-let-live approach is, in fact, one of the ways in which we define a community; if such rules and duties were not observed there would be no community.

From his birth every individual is being moulded by his parents and his community to follow the general lines of their way of life. Within this way of life broad provision is made for his needs and it orientates his ideals. It is rooted in the experiences of past generations, for, in any community, the process of passing on to the children the wisdom accumulated over its history is a necessary part of its way of life: otherwise the community would not survive.

The answers to all the problems the individual meets are not, of course, to be found ready made there, but the major problems which will face him have the general pattern of their solution laid down by convention, law, and morality. Thus when confronted with a particular moral problem he will not have to argue out for himself from first principles his course of action, but to reconcile any conflict in his desires and ideals within the appropriate part of the code of behaviour of his society.

To keep him in step with his society there are many forces acting on him. There will be usually strong legal or social sanctions against his conflicting with the way of life of other members of his society and strong positive attractions of security, approval, friendship and love to make him comply with it. Thus he will have grown up to act and think within its limits.

From their acceptance of duties and satisfactions deriving from the way of life, most people will gain, on balance, sufficient satisfactions not to wish to rebel against it, save in minor respects; some will not do so and will come into considerable conflict with their fellows: some will avoid such conflict but at the expense of transferring the conflict to within themselves. But only a small minority can normally come into open conflict with a society if it is to survive. To understand how such conflicts came about leads often, not so much to the condemnation of the individual alone, but of the whole set of circumstances which gave rise to conflict. The ordinary moral rules of a society may thus be regarded as empirical generalizations derived from a way of life which has, by experience, been found, on balance, satisfactorily to meet the problems and desires, rational and irrational, of its members.

Provided they are sufficiently widely formulated many of these rules can be found to apply in all societies, but in each society they are subject to many qualifications and exceptions. Such rules may prescribe, for instance, the need to tell the truth, to remember one's promises and other commitments, etc. These rules, however, are not, even in our own society, absolute; for instance, we do not regard the inventions of fiction nor many conventional and often quite insincere ways of heading and ending letters as lies, while social life generally would be completely inhibited if we were always to be strictly truthful; to know where to be tactful rather than truthful and vice versa are high social accomplishments. Thus the circumstances where these general prescriptions apply can be ascertained on no *a priori* principles, but only when one has a thorough knowledge of the way of life or the society concerned; nor usually can such conventions seriously be considered immoral. Thus important as rules are in understanding the way of life of the community, it is very easy to over-estimate their importance in the way of life of the individual. In our everyday intercourse we tend to think not nearly so much of general principles as of personal relations, according to learned patterns of behaviour. Whatever general rules we may learn, it is only through our experience of actually living in the society that we learn when they apply; and when we are thoroughly aware of the conventions of the society, though the rule may remain in the background of our minds, we much more usually decide our actions in the light of those conventions without any reference to the rule at all.

Now, although we have so far spoken broadly about 'ways of life', there are within a way of life a number of subsidiary and constituent patterns of personal relationships of an enduring nature. Such institutions are the family, the club, the crew of a ship or a religious body. These are, of course, organized on widely divergent lines. Each has its code of behaviour, and sometimes rules are laid down. These rules, however, are the minima for the functioning of the institution, and in practice are not normally much referred to; a club whose members did only what was required by the rules would very rapidly disintegrate. There are many thoroughly satisfactory members of institutions who have probably never read the rules—rather, they have learned from other members the conventions of the institution, including both their rights and obligations.

Institutions do, of course, link and interact; there are institutions within institutions—a committee is an institution within a club. A community is, itself, an institution. Thus, from his way of life as a whole, no less than from particular institutions within it, the individual must on balance gain some satisfaction, in order that it may have his support for its maintenance, and for him to continue to accept the associated duties and obligations.

Some ways of life are more coherent than others. This degree of coherence is evidenced by the way in which the duties and satisfactions, the ideals and the institutions, all supplement each other, the satisfactions of the one providing incentives for the duties of another; and the degree of incoherence is shown by their degree of unrelatedness, and at any rate potential conflict, though direct conflict may be avoided by the inevitable expedient of satisfying them at different times. Since these institutions exist primarily as patterns of behaviour in the minds of the individuals concerned, their coherencies and incoherencies are reflected there, too. Thus we would expect a fairly close relationship between the degree of coherence of the way of life and that of the outlook of individuals, and indeed, in so far as the individual is fully adapted to the way of life, we may regard them as the objective and subjective counterparts of each other.

There are, however, two other dimensions of the personality besides its degree of integration, as I indicated when we were considering psychology. These are a person's degree of adaptation to society and his degree of adjustment to his own needs. As we have seen, if a person is reasonably well adapted to the way of life of his society, its degree of integration will in large measure be reflected in his degree of integration. But however well integrated and adapted he may be, the way of life may still be ill adjusted to his own physical and psychological needs. Thus in some societies an individual may be reasonably fully adapted to his society only at the expense of great internal conflict and warping of his personality. A society whose way of life is ill adjusted to the needs of its members will thus increase the amount of conflict and the number of moral decisions they will have to face, and a society which is well adjusted will reduce the number.

Not everyone has accepted the absence of conflict as desirable. To show it is desirable ethically, we must distinguish first two different sorts of ethical problem. There is the problem of wrongdoing which is a result of genuine uncertainty as to what is the right course of action, and there is the problem of perversity or of weakness of will when the right course is known. The problem of knowing what is best to do in particular circumstances is simplified if the way of life is coherent and well integrated, and the more the scope of doubt is narrowed the better our ability is to forecast the consequences of each course open to us. So far as the individual is concerned this plainly puts a premium on intelligence, experience, understanding and lack of prejudice.

Perversity and weakness of will, when the right course is known, plainly present a different problem. There is a natural tendency for moral tenacity and strength of will in overcoming hardships and temptations to be praised. But such hardships and temptations themselves tend to get caught up in the praising and to be regarded as themselves somehow desirable. For, it may be said, if I know what I should do and do it, if not as a matter of habit, at least without any conflict, and because it accords with my wishes, then my action can hardly be regarded as having any very great moral merit. If I do the same thing but only after a great effort of will and in the face of great temptation not to do it or to choose an alternative course, then the merit is higher.

Now clearly, in judging such actions as right or

wrong, we are applying objective standards. Viewed subjectively the matter will be different. The man who is in harmony with his society will be able to channel his desires and interests in a way that is generally acceptable. The man who is at odds with his society and its standards may find great conflicts arising within himself as he struggles to reconcile the demands of society and his own needs. The efforts of this man to do what is right and good may be far greater. Whether he succumbs or not may depend less on him than on the temptations to which he is subjected. If he succumbs it would be curious to say he is better than the man who has experienced none of these temptations. Yet whether he succumbed may have depended, not on him so much as on his environment, and the man who did not experience such temptations might have succumbed much more easily. Thus the man who struggled hardest but gave way must, on this basis, be adjudged worse than the man who was of weaker moral fibre and was not tempted. This implies if ethical judgement is to be passed that whether a man is to be considered as good or bad, even when motives are taken into account, may depend on elements over which he has at best very partial control. This is a particularly unsatisfying result from the point of view of ethics.

We need not, of course, deny that the ability to do the right thing in the face of hardship and temptation is praiseworthy, but, nevertheless, we have no need to regard such temptations and conflicts as good in themselves. It is of interest to find Brunner, one of the foremost continental theologians, saying that 'Duty and genuine goodness are mutually exclusive. Obedience due to a sense of unwilling constraint is bondage and indeed the bondage of sin. If I feel I ought to do right it is a sign I cannot do it. If I could really do it there would be no question of "ought" about it at all.'[1] Perhaps, then, paradoxically we may regard the ideally virtuous individual in an ideal society as one who has normally no need to face a moral conflict of this type, but who does what is right without internal conflict, and with full understanding of the implications and consequences of his action.

This conclusion is borne out in another way. Clearly selfishness, the disproportionate emphasis on self in all its aspects, must in any society be regarded as immoral. This has led many people to think that its opposite, selflessness, is the ideal at which we must aim, and this idea has found support in asceticism, some of the psychological origins of which we have already mentioned. The logical conclusion of selflessness, however, is death by voluntary deprivation, and this can hardly be regarded as a very satisfactory ideal, quite apart from any question of its unnaturalness.

There is, however, a third course which lies open to us, whereby we judge situations in which we are involved neither entirely from the point of view of our own interests, nor yet from the point of view of everyone else while excluding our own interests, but from a point of view from which the self is transcended and from which the privileged position of oneself is treated

[1] *Natural Theology*, p. 74.

simply as not relevant. In other words the person judging must so consider the situation that the placing of anyone else in exactly his position in the situation would not affect the judgement. This interpretation places a premium on dispassionate and detached understanding, and yet allows for, and indeed, necessarily implies, within the very conception of understanding, full scope for compassion, which, with its emphasis on sharing the feelings and thought of others, is necessarily involved in it. This approach to a situation is also, of course, completely just.[1]

The word which may come to mind at this point is the word 'love'. But this is a word which covers a number of different and distinguishable states of mind, though in any one case they may be combined in any number of ways. For example the strong physical attraction of a woman for a man is very different from the emotional dependence of a child on its mother. Yet both come under the term 'love'. Further, the state of emotional dependence of one person on another is in no way limited to childhood, though it is to be regarded as a sign of immaturity and of failure to achieve satisfactory personal adjustment. It nevertheless forms a basis for many marriages including a high proportion of unsatisfactory ones.

[1]Since this essay cannot hope to be comprehensive we shall not be able to discuss further the vital question of justice, nor that of punishment, save to say that, on this interpretation of ethics we must regard motives of revenge as morally wrong. Rather we must conceive of punishment as that which is necessary when the circumstances are understood as completely and compassionately as possible, to reform and deter: factors which in themselves may not, of course, be easy to balance.

Very different from this state of emotional dependence is 'love' in the sense in which it applies here. This is the kind of open-hearted affection, fellow-feeling, understanding and compassion that can be freely given only by a very mature and well adjusted person. Used in this way the term is not to be associated by contrast with hatred or fear or guilt as a state of emotion, but, unlike these, it is to be regarded as a state of no emotion and so as completely rational. In this sense, clearly, love is a term which is fully applicable to the state which I wish to describe. In the most ultimate sense it is man's natural state of mind; it is fundamental in a sense in which other emotional and affective states are not. Indeed, it is the state of no emotion.

In short that attitude of mind which we must consider most moral belongs to someone who has a very wide and deep understanding and who, however much he may be personally involved in a situation, is not emotionally involved in it in such a way as to distort his understanding of any of the relationships involved, whether within himself or between himself and others. If this conception is correct, such an ideal individual would have high intelligence, powerful imagination and wide experience, emotionally as well as otherwise; he would, to use the terms I employed earlier, be fully adapted and fully integrated, and he would be internally entirely adjusted and secure, for no one who is uncertain of himself and internally insecure is able to take a dispassionate view of a situation in which he is himself involved. Such an individual is obviously closely comparable to the ideally 'normal' man—the ideal humanist—whose portrait, derived from the quite different field of psychology, we have already sketched. In other words, the person who, from the point of view of psychology is at one with himself is also the person who would be at one with his fellow men—if they let him be. Clearly such an individual would fit in more easily in some societies than in others. This leads us to discuss the moral criteria by which we can judge societies.

Appendix to Chapter XXII

If we bear in mind the crudity of the super-ego which we have already discussed, and our findings on ethics in the present chapter, I think we shall find ourselves in general agreement with the eight ways which Prof. Flugel in his book *Man Morals and Society* has suggested by which the crudity of the super-ego can be improved upon. These eight ways are:

(1) *From Egocentricity to Sociality*—in other words increasing respect, sympathy and eventually love for others.

(2) *From Unconscious to Conscious*—allowing for higher ideals and greater discrimination in their application, while allowing habit, etc., to direct action in more routine situations.

(3) *From Autism to Realism*—in other words, transition from, for instance, day dreaming or wishful thinking to the facts of reality.

(4) *From Moral Inhibition to Spontaneous 'Goodness'.*

(5) *From Aggression to Tolerance and Love.*

(6) *From Fear to Security.*

(7) *From Heteronomy to Autonomy*—in other words greater emphasis on individual responsibility and discrimination than reliance on the views of others, on convention, law, etc.

(8) *From Orectic (Moral) Judgement to Cognitive (Psychological) Judgement.* In other words a transition from passing of moral judgements on people to understanding them.

XXIII

The Comparison of Societies

FROM the point of view of psychology, the ideal individual is one who is completely adjusted, in the sense that all his internal and unconscious conflicts have been resolved: in other words he is at one with himself. That this is also necessary if he is to be ideally moral was one of the conclusions of the last chapter. But plainly, so far as morals are concerned, a great deal must depend upon his fellows, for any system of morals is essentially a system of values accorded to inter-personal relationships. We thus need some criterion for distinguishing, from the point of view of morals, the patterns of behaviour of different societies. We all believe that some societies and institutions are morally worse than others, but it seems difficult to apply ordinary ethical concepts, which are essentially applic-able to the judgement of individuals within a society, to societies themselves.

Societies are, however, in their nature, groups of individuals co-operating for survival and for the enjoyment of life according to a complex and enduring pattern of behaviour. This pattern of behaviour is ultimately in the minds of the individuals. It may to a greater or lesser extent have been codified, but this has normally derived from the pattern of behaviour of the individuals involved and not vice versa. What I am discussing, then, is the criteria, from the point of view of ethics and psychology, by which we may judge one complex pattern of behaviour as against another.

Now plainly, from what I have said before, we must expect such a pattern to be fairly closely adapted to the psychology of the people who follow it. The more the psychology of any considerable proportion of these people is warped, the more the pattern of behaviour which they follow will tend also to be warped, and vice versa; and as children grow up in more or less the same mould, their personalities too will be warped accordingly.

Now, a person with an authoritarian cast of mind will be well adapted to an authoritarian society, but as we have seen he will be the subject of considerable conflict within his own mind. The less authoritarian the individual becomes the less will be his own internal conflicts; but if he is to remain fully adapted to his society, the less authoritarian the society will have to be, too. It becomes then an empirical question to decide what changes in a pattern of behaviour will tend to reduce these conflicts and bring it more closely into accord with the needs of ideally normal individuals. This, then, suggests that the first criterion by which we may judge a society is by the extent to which those of its members who are well adapted to the way of life, are themselves well adjusted to the needs of their own personalities.

In practice, of course, within any society there is not one pattern of behaviour but many: behaviour at work or at home, at birth or death, at courting or at worship: all of these are more or less detailed patterns of behaviour, the main lines of which, having been learned, remain engraven, though by no means unchangeably so, in the mind of the individual and are followed as occasion demands. Such patterns of behaviour can, as I have indicated, make quite different and incompatible demands on the individual.

In practice they can be reconciled, because they have to be followed at different times, but clearly there is the possibility of great difficulties here. It has for instance long been recognized that one of the major causes of delinquency in children and of their failure to form stable moral attitudes is a rift between parental authorities. We can see how this arises every day in our own society: the man who works in a shop may be expected to be deferential to all customers, no matter how trying or unreasonable they may be: at home a quite different and perhaps objectionable personality may appear; a third may appear at his club or in the public house where he meets his friends, and a fourth, again quite different, may appear at church where he is churchwarden. If, then, there are potentially conflicting patterns of behaviour which the individual is expected to follow, since these patterns reside in his own mind, they will tend to produce and reflect conflict there.

Plainly, then, there is a close relationship between the extent to which a society is integrated, and the extent to which it is adjusted to the needs of the individual. In the ideal they would coincide. But since the ordinary society is far from the ideal, the degree of coherence of the society must be separately distinguished from the degree of adjustment. Further, the more closely the duties of an individual and his satisfactions are interwoven, the less onerous will be the way of life as a whole. Thus, if we are to satisfy the standards which have been set from the points of view both of psychology and ethics, it is plainly desirable that the way of life should be as fully integrated as possible, and this provides a second criterion by which we may judge a society.

These two criteria, although they are so abstract as I refer to them here, and although they may be refined and modified in the light of further knowledge, nevertheless provide objective criteria on which we may base our judgements of different ways of life. However, they are concepts which are of great complexity even when applied to the ways of life of small groups of individuals, and it is beyond the scope of any man to understand, even fairly fully, the way of life of more than a very few of his fellows. Further, even small changes in the way of life of a society may have very wide repercussions, and the more integrated is the way of life of the society the more extended will they be and thus the more difficult to forecast.

Nevertheless, I can still indicate in very general terms the direction in which such changes should be made.

XXIV

The Aims of Society

I HAVE so far shown that there are two criteria by which we may reasonably prefer one society to another —the internal adjustment of the personality of its members and the integration of its way of life. I must now briefly attempt to relate these criteria to the judgement of changes in the way of life of a society.

Even in an ideal society there would be need for government to manage and co-ordinate the affairs of its members, and for our everyday societies this is still its fundamental task. There has to-day, however, been grafted on to this concept of government another concept: the idea that the function of government is also to take active measures to improve the lot of its members and to increase their happiness by satisfying their interests and desires.

Though this looks on first sight a very reasonable programme for any government, it has certain grave shortcomings. It is really but a form of the subjective approach to ethics whose inadequacies we referred to earlier. But, since in various guises this theory underlies many contemporary ideals, a further elaboration of the objections to it seems warranted.

On the simplest approach to the theory each person has his own desires and interests and these are to be reconciled with those of other people. But what other people? Are the desires and interests of each person to be regarded as equal? Must I reconcile my desires and interests with those of a thief who breaks into my house? Plainly we cannot give equal weight to the desires and interests of each and every person irrespective of the interests of the community. We cannot have a community built on bilateral bargains. Inexorably we are driven to select the desires and interests of some group or proportion of the people as our standard whenever all are not agreed. This then becomes our standard and criterion. Suppose we then put forward some such standard group of people selected for their qualities, or position or interests or anything else. We are then faced with a not less intractable problem, for we have to establish some further criterion by which to justify the selection of the people in relation to whom our criterion is defined.

Suppose, however, we adopt as our criterion the interests and desires of the majority of the people concerned in any problem (though this too would require justification). The criterion by which we effect reconciliation is that aims and desires of the majority must have precedence. If Smith Minor and Jones Major express a desire for the sweets which Barker Minor has just bought, and if no one else is interested, Barker Minor will be morally bound to hand them over. Thus, we arrive at the position where strictly, the minority has no rights.

There is another facet to this thesis. In any consideration of the reconciling of interests and desires, we wish to improve the *status quo*. As our touchstone we must either use those interests and desires which passingly occur to the people concerned, or else we must use some more ultimate criterion to establish which are of more permanent value. Now on the subject of passing desires as, in another context, Professor Michael Oakeshott has reminded us recently, what Lord Acton said of the first Lord Liverpool is applicable—'the secret of his policy was that he had none'; and a Frenchman said of him that if he had been present at Creation he would have said, 'Mon Dieu, conservons le chaos'. A policy prescribed by the satisfying only of passing desires could lead only to chaos. Yet what more ultimate guide can we have to man's aims and desires? Even when his aims and desires have been ascertained, we have no criterion to say that one is more valuable, significant or important than another, for to have such a criterion would bring us back to the beginning of our problem.

If, instead of considering the promotion and reconciliation of aims and desires, we consider the promotion of happiness itself, similar difficulties arise. There is, for instance, the serious question of whose happiness should have priority. But there are other objections, which are perhaps more fundamental, which we can show by considering unhappiness.

The causes of unhappiness fall into two broad groups: there are those deriving directly from the environment of the individual, such as hunger or the tyranny of a nagging wife; and those which derive directly from the personality of the individual: as is clearly exemplified in the case of people who suffer from melancholia. Now in the first case it is often fairly easy to point to the obstacles to happiness, and the remedy to the immediate trouble, however difficult it may be to put into practice, is usually in its broad lines clear. In the second type of case the unhappiness springs from some lack of adjustment of the individual and again, though we may not know the remedy, we can, given a careful enough psychological study, at any rate usually diagnose the causes of the trouble, and sometimes do something to ease them.

But in neither case are we directly promoting happiness. We are attempting to remove specific causes of unhappiness—which is by no means the same thing.

In general, it would seem that normally there is very little we can do to promote happiness, as such. As with love (in the sense in which we used it earlier), happiness would seem to be the natural state when the obstacles to it are removed. Further, though happiness may be a state, it is not in itself a state at which we can aim, for it is normally a by-product of complete and contented absorption in the practical affairs of life.

Now, if this is correct, the second function of government to which I referred above, should properly be regarded not as promoting the happiness of the members of its society, but as attempting to remove specific causes of unhappiness.

In these circumstances, however, it is plainly no use laying down a blue-print for happiness in advance, for if happiness is a by-product of the everyday living of a satisfying way of life, it must plainly be the purpose of the blue-print to establish such a satisfactory way of life. This, however, is an extremely personal matter in which it is quite impossible to disregard either heredity or past environment, and to start afresh. It is very reasonable to point out that if environmental conditions are unsatisfactory, it is much more difficult to achieve a satisfying way of life; and certainly government can do a good deal about this. But government can do little, save in the most crude and uncertain way, directly to make more satisfying the accumulated instinctive and learned responses of each individual which in their interactions with the environment govern the way of life. For, once the basic needs of the body are satisfied, what matters above all in these responses is the pattern of personal relationships, and these are so complex that it will usually be impossible to forecast most of the repercussions of a change of the kind which falls within the scope of government.

If, however, the changes are such as to make the way of life better adjusted to the needs of the individuals, we shall, if these arguments are correct, be making changes which should certainly lead in the long run to an increase in happiness. But even theoretically this is not a simple matter, for it is to be noted that I have used the word 'adjusted' and not the word 'adapted'. This point requires elucidation.

If in a society in which the population is largely of authoritarian cast of mind, a strong authoritarian figure is removed, then his replacement after a lapse of time, and the chain of edicts, instructions, and exhortations which will follow, may well greatly increase the happiness of the people. The change will be one which make their way of life better adapted to their needs. They will now have someone they can put their trust in and obey implicitly, projecting on to him, and on to the scapegoats he will usually find, their own internal conflicts.

But a change of this nature does no more than provide an escape for such people from their own internal sense of persecution, and it will almost certainly be maintained at the expense of much unhappiness and misery on the part of many others. Thus it is probable that some Germans were actually happier when Hitler came to power: the loss of their freedom meant little to them when they had their Führer to obey.

Thus, though the coming into power of Hitler increased the happiness of some people, this is clearly no criterion of the moral value of the change. This was a change in the direction of better *adapting* the way of life to the needs of the people. We, however, are concerned with finding changes which will better *adjust* the way of life to the needs of the people: changes, in other words, which will lead to a reduction in the amount of conflict in the minds of the individuals, with a consequential reduction in the amount of irrational distortion of their personal relationships and their way of life. Clearly, the amount a government can do here is strictly limited, for it can rarely be much more enlightened than its people, when it is seeking to change, however little, their very cast of mind and outlook.

So indefinite is this criterion, in fact, that it may

quite reasonably be said that it is almost useless: and
without question its use is very limited. But, in fact,
changes in the direction of adjustment and integration are not brought about by government edict nor
by considering them in the light of any criterion: they
are brought about much more subtly, piecemeal, by
the resolution of the ordinary problems of everyday life
by ordinary people—always provided the changes are
made with reason, understanding and compassion. If
the changes are motivated thus, be they efforts to help
a single alcoholic or to frame legislation to deal with
delinquent children, then they will usually be changes
leading in the direction of better adjustment of those
concerned: they will be the right changes from good
motives for good ends.

There appears to be a further interesting implication to this thesis, though I cannot develop it here. In
a society where the cast of mind of most of the people
is warped and irrational, their conduct of the ordinary
business of life will be warped and irrational, too. The
whole way of life will thus be warped and irrational
and this will tend to maintain the irrationality and
warping of the people, and of younger generations as
they grow up in its mould. If, however, for some
reason the cast of mind or way of life becomes
markedly more rational and adjusted in some fields,
this should have repercussions in other fields and
should tend to start cumulative movements towards
greater adjustment and rationality. Needless to say,
however, all sorts of factors may intervene to check or
reverse this progress.

Finally, we come to the second and less important criterion by which we may judge changes in the way of life of a society. This, as we might expect, is that the change should lead to closer integration in the way of life. This, too, is necessary if a way of life is to prove really satisfying to its members, and it, too, is arrived at, not so much by government action or by choosing which changes should be made on the grounds that they promote closer integretation, but by the increase in genuineness, openness, friendship and understanding which I have already put forward as a psychological and ethical ideal. Not only, however, are these changes desirable from the point of view of psychology and ethics. They are also desirable, as I shall attempt to show, from the point of view of religion.

XXV

Religion and Society

I HAVE already described at some length some of the
basic characteristics of men's minds as revealed by
psycho-analysis and, in particular, I stressed the influence of the Super-Ego—the irrational conscience—
which so afflicts mankind, alienating each person from
himself, from his fellows, and from God. I showed the
profound influence of the parents, and more ultimately, of the way of life as a whole in moulding it. I
indicated the profound importance, where the irrational conscience is strong, of the process of projection
as a means of relieving men of the profound oppression
of irrational guilt. This process of projection, as we saw,
tends greatly to influence men's conception of God.

In the strong authoritarian environment in which
early Christianity grew up many irrational psychological traits combined to give a distinctive slant to
the teachings of the Church. Guilt, asceticism, self-
abasement, taboo, the fear of 'hubris', and the projection on to God of the two aspects of the parents, the
good, helpful and protective, and the cruel and frustrating, all have served to provide a conception of
God and of the ways in which we serve him, which,
while meeting the immediate needs of those concerned, tended constantly to distort men's understanding of him and of the necessary conditions for

the Good Life. So important has been the place given to sin and to guilt in Christianity, and so profound has been its influence on the whole way of life of Western society, that I must perforce consider it further.

The relationship of sin to morality has been a stumbling block even for Christian theologians,[1] as for them the sinfulness of all men derives from the Fall. This sinfulness is regarded as inherent in the nature of man and is thus something over which it is difficult to maintain he has any influence. On the other hand, it is no less difficult to say that a man can be morally guilty of something of whose sinfulness he was not aware and over which he had no control. Barth has accordingly taken the heroic course of completely rejecting morality, on the grounds that to follow the dictates of conscience is to give divine freedom to the individual. Brunner fails to find effective moral norms. Those he puts forward he finds in the laws, processes and orders of the world of nature and history and in the Holy Scriptures. But, as we noted earlier, to arrive at a moral conclusion, at least one of the premises must be moral and he fails to show why he 'ought' to adopt these norms. Neibuhr accepts the total depravity of man but adds to it the completely inconsistent uneasiness of a thoroughly bad conscience, for even in the terms of Christian theology, a doctrine of total depravity is untenable in that it provides no point of contact for God.

The doctrine of depravity has an important part in

[1]This paragraph and the next owe much to *Faith and Duty* by N. H. G. Robinson, Gollancz, 1950.

Christian doctrine for when it is rejected the doctrine of grace is endangered. On the other hand, it is difficult for the Christian theologian to postulate inequality of sin, for all men are regarded equally as sinners before the eyes of God. Yet, to assert that all men are equally sinful seems completely to repudiate the basis of all ordinary ethics. This is an interpretation which as Prof. Tennant observes 'would seem to make an end at once of ethics and Christian theology'. (*The Concept of Sin*, p. 265.) Further, to hold to the universality and totality of sin would seem to make an end to the idea of responsibility, which is equally vital to Christian doctrine. Thus the Christian theologian is faced with the task of reconciling the universality of sin and man's responsibility for it, and at the same time of combining the depth of that sin with some point of access for God in man. If men have it in their power to avoid sin, this casts doubts on its strict universality, yet if all men are equally sinful, then they must presumably be totally sinful and thus inaccessible to divine grace.

No generally acceptable reconciliation of these apparently irreconcilable ideas has been found. Yet, within the context of my arguments there is a sense in which they can be reconciled quite naturally.

In so far as the individual is at one with himself, so far is he necessarily at one with God, since, as I have attempted to show, pure consciousness is one with the ground of the universe; and since, for the Christian, God is good, when man is at one with God, so far is man good also. But since the state of being at one with oneself is an ideal which, in the nature of man can be approached, but hardly attained, and since, in so far as it is not attained, the individual is in conflict with himself and so with God, which is, of course, a state of sin, so far is the natural state of man sinful.

This sinfulness is clearly much more fundamental than the transgression of the ordinary rules of society; though there is a relationship between them, it is clearly not direct.

This interpretation of the nature of sin finds support from Tillich. 'The very heart of what classical Christianity has called "sin" is the unreconciled duality of ultimate and preliminary concerns, of the finite and that which transcends finitude, of the secular and the holy. Sin is the state of things in which the holy and the secular are separated, struggling with each other and trying to conquer each other. It is the state in which God is not "all in all", the state in which God is "in addition to" all other things.'[1]

It follows that in this sense self-castigation is hardly less sinful than those thoughts or actions which gave rise to it. Both may be equally characteristic of a mind which is alienated from God. The strong emphasis on moral perfection and irrational guilt at departure from it are hall marks of authoritarianism. As Tillich says 'The term "saint" has been misunderstood and distorted; saintliness has been identified with religious or moral perfection. Protestantism, for these reasons, has finally removed the concept of sainthood from theology and the reality of the saint from religion. But

[1] *Systematic Theology*, Vol. I, p. 242.

sainthood is not personal perfection. Saints are persons who are transparent for the ground of being which is revealed through them . . .'[1]

The fact that the concept of sin has come to be identified with departures from ordinary moral and religious perfection and has loomed so large in the preoccupations of the Christian churches, is but one example of the influence of the prevailing ways of life and casts of mind of those societies in which Christianity grew up and flourished. But the influence of society has, of course, been far more widespread than this, for most of the members of the Church have usually been full members of society: the beliefs, standards and ritual of the Church have thus become an integral part of their way of life, and their loves and hates, preoccupations and inhibitions have tended to be reflected in its teaching.[2]

Further, since to say anything about God in the literal sense of words is to say something false about him, and since he can be spoken about only symbolically or by analogy, the symbols and analogies used by the Church also have tended to be drawn from the everyday life of the people, and in part from their

[1]Op cit., p. 135.

[2]Nowhere has this been clearer than in the subject of sex, and to some extent in the attitude to women. Yet, as Tillich confirms 'Sexual desire is not evil as desire, and the breaking of conventional laws is not evil as the breaking of conventional laws, but sexual desire and sexual autonomy are evil if they bypass the centre of the other person . . . ' (Love, Power and Justice, p. 117.) Indeed the sexual union of two people, in so far as it leads to full and harmonious union of their personalities, leads past them to God, and this is true whether the union is within or without marriage.

pre-Christian past. This is not to suggest, of course, that these symbols are consciously worked out; such a suggestion would be quite misleading. Since we earlier discussed some of the characteristics and implications of symbolism, in particular in connexion with aesthetics, it will be apparent that the processes by which particular events became symbolic are so complex and their implications so abstruse that they must be regarded as deriving their meaning from all levels of the human psyche, conscious and unconscious, rational and irrational, superficial and profound: and the more powerful the symbol, the more likely it is to have some of its roots of meaning in the deepest levels of the psyche, some of which may be repressed and rejected by the conscious mind.

To enter this profoundly important and fascinating, though very controversial, field of symbolism is, however, something which I cannot do here, not least because so much of it lies as yet very inadequately explored. The works of Jung do, however, provide some glimpses into the extremely complex web of meanings which lie beneath the formulations of doctrines and practices of the great religions of the world and which have in the past given their symbols such deep and compelling significance.[1]

This relationship of religious symbolism to society brings out once more the impossibility of adequately considering any religion apart from its members, and since its members normally form a community of

[1]See also A. W. Watts, *Myth and Ritual in Christianity*, Thames & Hudson, 1953.

greater or smaller dimensions, and their very lives depend upon the maintenance of that community, the Church inevitably tends to get associated with this need to maintain society, and its values and its teachings tend to get emphasized and deflected accordingly. These pressures are, of course, inevitable and give rise to many difficulties when the way of life of the society changes, and the Church finds itself under pressure to support transient aspects of the way of life at the expense of matters which are of ultimate significance: as witness the views of certain clergy in favour of the maintenance of the death penalty.

It follows, however, from the arguments I have been putting forward that in every man and woman there is need for love, and ultimately a need to resolve internal and external conflicts, and so to become at one with themselves, with their fellow-men and with God. We may therefore regard it as the primary function of religion to keep clear these objectives and to guide the way of life of all its members in this direction. The diversions are many and only exceptionally have these ends been clearly seen. Yet the fundamental insights that are here in question are not new in the history of mankind. This I shall attempt most briefly to indicate in the next chapter by reference to a few of the most fundamental tenets of the Christian faith; but of course their detailed application I cannot here pursue.

XXVI

The Relationship to Christianity

IN the first essay in this book I attempted to show that it was necessary, in order to understand the everyday world, to postulate a non-physical medium or ground of the universe—being-itself or God. In so doing I adduced a variety of evidence, including the reports of the full mystical union with God, though there are other forms of revelation, too. These more or less clear insights have formed the basis of all the major religions of the world. In various ways I have already given indications of this; and I may elucidate the point further by giving a very brief indication of the way in which some of the basic tenets of Christianity coincide with what I have been saying so far in this book.

Revelation is the term used in the Christian Church to describe a variety of special and unusual insights into the underlying nature of our being, and of the universe—insights into an order which is ultimate and which is hidden from our everyday eyes. Such revelation may be original inspiration, such as that associated with the mystical experience, or, on the other hand, it may derive from symbols.

Natural events like birth and death can be the bearer of revelation; so can all manner of ordinary experiences such as sex or dreams. The written and spoken word have been of enormous importance in giving rise to revelatory experiences. In particular the teachings and services of the Church are revealing of the divine mystery, being symbolic through and through. Likewise the personalities of others can be the bearer of revelation in so far as they are transparent to the ground of being which is revealed through them. In all these cases, that which gives rise to the revelatory experience points beyond itself to a deeper and more profound significance.

For Christianity the revelation in Jesus as the Christ is the final revelation. This claim is basic to the Christian Churches. The term 'final', however, has given rise to a great deal of misunderstanding. It means more than the last: 'It means the decisive, fulfilling, unsurpassable revelation, that which is the criterion of all the others. This is the Christian claim, and this is the basis of a Christian theology.'[1]

But the original revelations in the life of Christ and those who came in contact with him must be distinguished from the revelations stemming from these original revelations, which for succeeding generations have been symbolic.

The Christian churches claim that Christ was the perfect man, being also one with God. In the terms of the arguments which I have been putting forward, we would thus expect Christ, when he attained maturity, to have attained the psychological and ethical ideal of being at one with himself, and with God, and to have been characterized by open-heartedness, understanding

[1]Tillich. *Systematic Theology*, Vol. I, p. 148.

and compassion; to have been a completely adjusted and integrated personality, though necessarily ill-adapted to his environment.

That these were his characteristics is borne out graphically in the New Testament. His maintenance of unity with God 'is clear in the Gospel reports about the unbreakable unity of his being with that of the ground of all being, in spite of his participation in the ambiguities of human life'.[1]

But through his very perfection, there was the risk that Jesus, the man, would himself become the object of worship.[2] Accordingly it was essential that Jesus should renounce everything that could have benefited him personally—everything, indeed, that was finite about him, in order that he should be fully transparent to the divine mystery. As Tillich says 'Jesus of Nazareth is the medium of the final revelation because he sacrifices himself completely to Jesus as the Christ.'

But the Church regards Jesus not only as the Christ, Messiah or 'anointed one'; he is also identified with the 'Logos' which is both 'reason' and the continuous immanent principle of order in the Universe. The basis of this doctrine is the claim that the Logos became flesh, that the principle of divine self-revelation became manifest in the event 'Jesus as the Christ'.[3]

[1]Tillich. Op cit., p. 151.

[2]A risk which appears to be particularly prevalent at the present time.

[3]The identification of Christ with 'Logos' can, perhaps, be explained more fully as follows:

Logos is the continuous immanent principle of order in the universe—the power which manifests itself in the behaviour which constitutes the physical world. The physical body of

As Tillich says, 'The Logos, the principle of all divine manifestation, becomes a being in history under the conditions of existence, revealing in this form the basic and determinative relation of the ground of being to us, symbolically speaking, the "heart of the divine life".'[1] The Logos is, of course, that aspect of God which is spoken of symbolically as the 'Son of God'. Accordingly the 'only-begotten Son of God' was not originally Jesus, the son of Mary, but before his incarnation as Jesus, was simply the Word (Logos) and Wisdom (Sophia) of God—the creative power by which the world was made. Thus whether we think of Jesus as the perfect man at one with God, or simply as an aspect of God, his unity with God remains.

Further, since time is a relationship deriving from change in the physical world which is, of course, one aspect of God, time does not apply to God himself. God is eternal in that he is outside time. As a symbol of eternal life, Christianity uses the resurrection: likewise, immortality is life in God and outside time.

There are many other aspects of God which are symbolically distinguished. Thus when God is spoken of as the Father this symbolizes the continuous dependence and unity of man with the divine ground.

Jesus was one of its manifestations and Jesus, the man, experienced all its vicissitudes.

But Jesus was the perfect man, completely at one with himself, and so, since pure consciousness is one with the ground of the universe, or God, he was completely at one with God. Thus that aspect of God which is Logos became incarnate in Jesus.

[1]Op. cit., p. 175.

The balancing concept of God as Lord, on the other hand, emphasizes his unapproachable majesty and glory. 'Almighty God' refers to his all-pervading and prevailing creative power; 'eternal God' to the unchanging nature of the ground of the Universe.

Also profoundly important in Christianity is the conception of God as love. I have already shown how a growth of open-heartedness, fellow-feeling, affection —the growth of the ability to give and receive love, in short—is natural in an individual as he approaches the ideal state of mind in which all internal conflicts are resolved, and he is at one with himself, with his fellow-men and with God. In such a case the individual who has been alienated from God is reunited with him. It is this deep longing and its fulfilment, in communion whether with God or our fellows, which in this fundamental sense is called love. But since God is the ground of all being, man's love of his fellows is, in a sense, itself love of God; and also, man's love of God is the love with which God loves himself, for God is both subject and object. Thus the distinctions within God, including the infinity of finite forms, are separated and reunited in the eternal process of the divine life which is divine love.

All these are ascriptions to God which are implicit in, and completely in harmony with all that I have been saying of the nature of God—of the medium. Further, once the Universe is seen as a manifestation of God then all aspects of life are revealing of his presence.

XXVII

Some Further Comments and Speculations on Psychic Phenomena

IN the earlier note on psychic phenomena (Chapter VIII) I indicated that one mind is distinguished from another mind neither by time nor by space, and that it is presumably distinguished by its own particular continuity of experience, by its memories, and by its own preoccupations with what is happening in its own system. Accordingly I indicated that it appeared that the major reason preventing one mind from establishing contact with another mind by para-normal means, is the difficulty of actually breaking through the preoccupations of that mind. When this difficulty is overcome, telepathy occurs.

Now as a result of consideration of the relationship of mental to physical events, I arrived at the conclusion that physical events can be regarded as the forms and patterns of the behaviour of the medium abstracted by our sensory system from the medium itself; whereas mental events are the medium conditioned by the behaviour. I assumed that the physical counterparts of mental events occur in the brain. We may, of course, grant that it is there that the constantly interlocking and developing sequence of events which constantly preoccupies us, takes place. But mental events are not themselves located in the brain, for location does not apply to them. Accordingly it would seem that there is no reason why physical events taking place elsewhere should not be experienced as mental events, if the attention can be diverted to them from the ordinary flow of mental events reaching us by the senses. There is, in fact, strong evidence that this happens in clairvoyance.[1]

If, however, a person can experience as a mental event, physical events which occur elsewhere than in his brain, the question arises whether he can modify their sequence. He can do so in his own brain, so presumably he can do so elsewhere since neither time nor space apply to mental events. There is strong evidence to bear out this suggestion. This has been found in a number of experiments, notably with dice. A sequence of throws can be so altered as to produce results which are widely different from the results to be expected by chance. The influence on any individual throw may be very slight, but over a long sequence of throws, it becomes statistically of great significance. Of course, not all people are able to control and project their minds in this way; some are able to do it better than others and many cannot succeed at all. But where mind control has been cultivated to very great extremes, as in the case with Yogins, instances are reported where the influence of mind over matter is quite spectacular. And, of course,

[1] If I am correct in the suggestion (to which I refer later) that all physical events have 'mental' counterparts, telepathy becomes a sub-class of clairvoyance since telepathy refers only to the experience by one person of mental events occurring in the mind of another.

the supreme examples in this context are the miracles of Christ, whose mind was completely at one with itself and so with God, and whose control over his own mind was accordingly perfect.

Pre-cognition gives rise to yet other problems. But, as I have indicated, neither physical nor mental events occur in time. From the point of view of an ordinary observer, individual physical events occur in the great sequence of events which constitutes the physical universe, and from which the concept of time is derived. The sequence of mental events, however, is not so limited. In exceptional circumstances we can experience mental events whose physical counterparts, not only are occurring elsewhere than in our brains, but also, whose physical counterparts (when related by an observer to the normal sequence of physical change) occurred in the past or are yet to occur in the future. There is much evidence, both from experimental and spontaneous phenomena, to bear this out.

At this point the question arises as to the bearing of these suggestions on immortality. That the developing sequence of mental events, which each one of us is, should (from the point of view of a temporal observer) remain in existence outside time, notwithstanding the ending of the development of the sequence with death, is to be expected from what I have been saying; for time does not limit mental events. There are, however, a number of cases on record which seem to imply that not only does the personality endure after death, but that it can remain active. Apparently dead persons have communicated with living persons in ways too complex to lend themselves to any other interpretation.[1] This also would seem to be not inconsistent with what we have been saying. Indeed, if the personality endures after death, its influence might be felt in diverse ways, for it would no longer be preoccupied by the constant flow of events reaching it by the senses.

We may, then, ask if all men survive equally. Perhaps at least part of the answer is to be found by considering what was said earlier about the nature of sin —the state in which man is in conflict with and alienated from himself and from God. Not only the greater the degree of conflict, the narrower is the range of consciousness, and the less wide and rich are the mental experiences to survive, but also the less full is the mastery of the individual over himself. And if such mastery existed before death, there appears no reason to assume that after death it does not continue[2] to exist outside time. Exceptionally a personality possessing such control during life[3] may make its presence felt after death by influencing the minds of living people, or by affecting the sequence of physical events. But

[1] See, for example, G. N. M. Tyrell—*The Personality of Man*—Chapter 17, on 'Cross-correspondences'.

[2] The word 'continue' is, of course, a temporal word, as are many other of the terms used in this chapter, though the context strictly requires a non-temporal term. This is, I think, a difficulty inherent in language; it can perhaps to some extent be met by adding the words 'from the point of view of an ordinary observer', but I have not wished to encumber the text by adding this when the meaning seemed clear.

[3] In this context it is hardly necessary to add that the supreme example of a person having mastery over his own mind is, of course, Jesus.

of course the mind of the person being influenced may be more or less receptive, and in particular, unconscious mental processes akin to dream-work may operate to change the form of the ideas reaching consciousness.[1]

Which people, then, are likely to be most susceptible to receiving extra-sensory impressions? Apparently experimenters have not yet found any criteria by which they can forecast which people or types of people would be likely to be successful, though they have established that the power is quite widespread among adults, as well as children, in all parts of the world.

It follows from what we have been saying in these essays that potentially everyone possesses this power. But the ability to keep the mind calm and sensitive and open to any impressions, is by no means common, and this would appear to be necessary if extra-sensory influences are to be experienced. There is some evidence to suggest that this is so. Where, however, a mind is subject to considerable subconscious or unconscious conflict, there is often a fairly constant flow of fantasy, more or less repressed, but liable to obtrude into consciousness if the attention is not otherwise constantly diverted. Accordingly, where there is such conflict, one would not expect the subject to be able to disengage his attention or to become aware of other than very compelling impressions: and, as I have said, where such impressions do break through, as in times of crisis, one might expect some

[1]See G. N. M. Tyrell—*Apparitions*, Duckworth, rev. edn. 1953.

unconscious process akin to dream-work to take place. This seems a possible explanation of certain apparitions.

On similar grounds to these speculations, one might expect the power of receiving extra-sensory impressions to be found in very young children, in whom any firm pattern of mental conflict has not become established. This seems to me to be possibly a significant element in the building up of the super-ego in children. Likewise, it seems possible *prima facie* that extra-sensory powers would be found among very primitive peoples, for whom the separation of the everyday physical world from the 'great whole' is much less complete than it is with us. And of course, there is much evidence that they do have these powers.

Finally, I may attempt to reformulate, as concisely as possible, the ultimate, if tentative, conclusion of these essays. It will be recalled that, in the first part of this book, I noted that the work of the Phenomenalists and of psychologists had drawn attention to the fact that our idea of the physical world is built up from the organization of, and relations between, sense-data. In this sense, mental events are more fundamental than physical events. I also suggested that our concepts of time and space are similarly derived. Furthermore, I showed that our sensory mechanisms are such that only forms and patterns are relayed from the world around us. These forms are the forms taken by the medium, but abstracted from the medium itself. They condition the forms of electrical events in the neuronal networks of the cortex; these we experience as mental events.

These physical counterparts of mental events, I also showed, are apparently not essentially different from any other physical events. This gives some grounds for suggesting that all physical events, whether experienced or not, have 'mental' counterparts. With the idea of mental events of which we are not conscious, psycho-analysis has made us familiar, and, on the other hand, there is much evidence to suggest that the physical counterparts of mental events need not necessarily occur in the brain, but can be located remotely in space and time.

There would seem grounds, then, for suggesting that physical events are merely an aspect—the form— of mental events—of which we ourselves are but a developing sequence. Such events, as I have tried to show, are occurring in the medium—in God. Thus in the ultimate I arrive at the tentative conclusion that physical events are the forms of a developing sequence of ideas in the mind of God.

XXVIII

Conclusions

I MAY now summarize very briefly the arguments
which I have put forward in the preceding pages in
this part of the book. I attempted to show:

(1) In the ordinary course of establishing associations which forms a fundamental part of the
learning process certain associations are set up
which are not cognitive but are instead of a
strong emotional nature. Whenever these are
evoked, since the equilibrium of the organism
tends thereby to be disturbed, the cognitive
responses tend to be distorted in order to obviate
this, and great internal conflicts may thereby be
set up.

(2) In almost everyone these warpings and distor-
tions are present in some measure. Our ability
to discern them we owe largely to psycho-
analysis, which has also brought out clearly the
desirability of reducing their intensity.

(3) We are accordingly able to postulate a psychologically ideally 'normal' mind which is fully
adjusted and in which there are no longer
internal conflicts, and which is internally secure
—a mind, in short, which is at one with itself.

(4) The characteristics of such a 'normal' person are
more or less those of an ideal humanist. He will

be completely rational, completely open and genuine, and will be receptive, understanding and compassionate.

(5) He stands in strong contrast to the mal-adjusted person, who, though his mal-adjustment may take many forms, will tend to be irrational, to hide his real personality from himself, as well as others, behind one or many masks, and who will tend to be prejudiced, unreceptive and insensitive.

(6) One particularly common and significant form of such warping is the 'authoritarian' type of personality which tends to be repressed, conventional and rigid, with little capacity for love and strong tendency to seek and admire power and obedience to power.

(7) Where this is the prevailing cast of mind, it tends to be reflected in all walks of life, and in particular in strongly patriarchal households, and in strongly authoritarian politics and religion.

(8) Such a way of life may be well integrated, but it is very ill-adjusted to the needs of those who follow it, however well adapted to it they may be.

(9) These three factors: adjustment, integration and adaptation, are of the greatest importance in considering an individual and his way of life; and since the way of life has its counterpart in the learned responses of the individual, the concept of the degree of adjustment and of

integration can be applied to each. Adaptation is a measure of the extent to which the individual fits in with his way of life.

(10) In the chapters on ethics we found that right means, good motives and good ends were all equally important in arriving at an ethical judgement.

(11) Such standards derive in the first instance from the way of life, though in practice the way of life of ordinary people will often deviate from the rather idealized version which is currently accepted as desirable.

(12) Some ways of life are ethically (and psychologically) better than others; the criteria being the extent to which they are adjusted and integrated.

(13) In so far as changes are sought in a way of life these should be their criteria, too, and so far will they lead to greater spontaneity and happiness. Changes in our everyday relationships which are made rationally and with full understanding, yet compassionately, tend to modify the way of life in this direction.

(14) This is borne out in another way. In any society, selfishness, which tends to break up the society, is condemned. The ethically ideal counterpart of this is not abnegation but that attitude of mind in which the self is given no special consideration. This is a fully rational, understanding, dispassionate yet compassionate attitude of mind—the attitude of love.

(15) We accordingly arrive at the ideal situation in which psychologically and ethically the ideal individual in an ideal society is at one with himself and with his fellow men. In such circumstances, he will also be at one with God.

(16) Thus, if rightly understood, sin is not to be conceived of as a departure from the ethical and religious ideals of society but as an alienation from God and from the roots of one's own being. This conception has, however, been much warped by authoritarian tendencies in the Church and in society.

(17) Properly speaking, indeed, the Church should not be juxtaposed against society, for it is one aspect of society and of the way of life of the men and women who are its members.

(18) The close link between the way of life and religion is borne out by the ways in which we speak of God symbolically, for the symbols draw their significance from the way of life, as well as from all levels of men's being, down to the very depths.

(19) Finally, when we come to look at the basic significance of the fundamental tenets of Christianity, we find that these fully bear out what I have attempted to show in this book:

'The Heavens declare the Glory of God and the firmament showeth his handiwork.'

'The law of the Lord is perfect, converting the soul: The testimony of the Lord is sure, making simple the wise.'

A BRIEF BIBLIOGRAPHY

I READ or consulted a very large number of books and articles while formulating and recording the views set out in these essays. Some of the books to which I am particularly indebted are listed below for anyone who wishes to read further about the subjects I have touched on. Almost all the books should be intelligible to those who are not specialists in the subjects with which they deal. With very few exceptions they have all been published since 1939.

Chapter II

E. D. Adrian—*The Physical Background of Perception*, Oxford, 1947 (and Chapters VI and VII).
A. J. Ayer—*The Foundations of Empirical Knowledge*, Macmillan, 1940.
F. A. Hayek—*The Counter-Revolution in Science*, Free Press, 1952.
P. Laslett (Ed.)—*The Physical Basis of Mind*, Blackwell, 1950.
H. Margerau—*The Nature of Physical Reality*, McGraw Hill.
H. H. Price—*Perception*, Oxford, 2nd edn., 1950.
E. Schrödinger—*Science and Humanism*, C.U.P., 1951 (and in Chapter IV).

Chapter III

L. Barnett—*The Universe and Dr. Einstein*, Gollancz, 1949.
H. Dingle—*Through Science to Philosophy*, Oxford, 1937.
A. Einstein—*Relativity* (14th and 15th edn.), Methuen, 1955.
P. A. Schlipp (Ed.)—*Albert Einstein, Philosopher, Scientist*, Tudor, revised edn., 1951.
G. J. Whitrow—*The Structure of the Universe* (and in Chapter IV), Hutchinson.

Chapter IV

Viscount Samuel—*Essay in Physics*, Blackwell, 1951.
F. E. Simon and Others—*Low Temperature Physics*, Pergamon, 1952.

Chapter V

L. von Bertalanffy—*Problems of Life*, Watts, 1952.
J. A. V. Butler—*Man is a Microcosm*, Macmillan, 1950.
V. H. Mottram—*The Physical Basis of Personality*, Penguin, 1944.
E. Schrödinger—*What is Life?*, Cambridge, 1944.

204

Chapters VI and VII

J. C. Eccles—*The Neurophysiological Basis of Mind*, Oxford, 1953.
(Particularly Chapters VII and VIII.)
H. H. Price—*Thinking and Experience*, Hutchinson, 1953.
J. S. Wilkie—*The Science of Mind and Brain*, Hutchinson, 1953.
J. Z. Young—*Doubt and Certainty in Science*, Oxford, 1951.

Chapter VIII

J. B. Rhine—*The Reach of the Mind*, Penguin, 1954.
J. B. Rhine—*New Frontiers of the Mind*, Penguin, 1950.
G. N. M. Tyrrell—*The Personality of Man*, Penguin, 1946.
G. N. M. Tyrrell—*Apparitions*, Duckworth, 1952.

Chapters IX–XI

J. Custance—*Wisdom, Madness and Folly*, Gollancz, 1950.
W. R. Inge—*Mysticism in Religion*, Hutchinson.
F. S. C. Northrop—*The Meeting of East and West*, Macmillan,
New York, 1946.
S. Radhakrishnan—*Eastern Religions and Western Thought*, Oxford,
2nd edn., 1940.
E. Underhill—*Mysticism*, Methuen, 1912.
A. Waley—*The Way and Its Power*, Allen & Unwin, 1949.
Fung Yu-Lan—*The Spirit of Chinese Philosophy*, Kegan Paul,
Trench Trubner, 1947.

Chapter XII

Sir C. M. Bowra—'Inspiration and Poetry' (*The Rede Lecture*,
1951), Cambridge, 1951.
B. Ghiselin—*The Creative Process*, University of California Press,
1952.
S. K. Langer—*Philosophy in a New Key*, Harvard U.P., 1951.
S. K. Langer—*Meaning and Symbolism*, Routledge & Kegan Paul,
1953.
H. Osborne—*The Theory of Beauty*, Routledge & Kegan Paul,
1952.

Chapter XIII

E. E. Evans-Pritchard and Others—*The Institutions of Primitive
Society*, Blackwell, 1954.
H. Frankfort and Others—*Before Philosophy*, Penguin, 1949.

Chapter XV

E. Conze—*Buddhism*, Cassirer, 1951.

M. Hiriyanna—*The Essentials of Indian Philosophy*, Allen & Unwin, 1949.

C. Humphreys—*Buddhism*, Penguin, 1951.

R. C. Majumdar and A. D. Pusalker—*The Vedic Age*. Allen & Unwin, 1952.

S. Nikhilananda—*The Upanishads* (1st selection), Phoenix, 1951.

Chapters XVII–XX

R. B. Cattell—*An Introduction to Personality Study*, Hutchinson, 1950.

R. Dalbiez—*Psycho-Analytical Method and the Doctrine of Freud*, Longmans, 1941.

H. J. Eysenck—*The Uses and Abuses of Psychology*, Penguin, 1953.

J. C. Flugel—*Man, Morals and Society*, Duckworth, 1945.

E. Fromm—*The Fear of Freedom*, Routledge & Kegan Paul, 1942.

E. Fromm—*Psycho-Analysis and Religion*, Gollancz, 1951.

E. Fromm—*The Forgotten Language*, Gollancz, 1952.

P. McKellar—*A Textbook of Human Psychology*, Cohen & West, 1952.

R. E. Money-Kyrle—*Psycho-Analysis and Politics*, Duckworth, 1951.

N. Tinbergen—*The Study of Instinct*, Oxford, 1951.

Chapters XXI–XXIV

R. M. Hare—*The Language of Morals*, Oxford, 1952.

A. Macbeath—*Experiments in Living*, Macmillan, 1952.

M. Oakeshott—*Political Education*, Bowes & Bowes, 1951.

A. W. Prior—*Logic and the Basis of Ethics*, Oxford, 1949.

P. Tillich—*Love, Power and Justice*, Oxford, 1954 (and Chapter XXVI).

S. Toulmin—*The Place of Reason in Ethics*, Cambridge, 1950.

Chapter XXV

N. H. G. Robinson—*Faith and Duty*, Gollancz, 1950.

A. W. Watts—*Myth and Ritual in Christianity*, Thames & Hudson, 1953.

Chapter XXVI

P. Tillich—*Systematic Theology*, Vol. I, Nisbet, 1953.